Teacher's Guide and Answer Key

Structural Arithmetic II

Margaret Stern
Toni S. Gould

About the Authors

Margaret B. Stern is a graduate of Wellesley College and has a master's degree from the Bank Street College of Education. She spends much of her time training teachers of children with learning problems, lectures extensively, and conducts workshops throughout the United States and overseas. She has been a special lecturer at many universities, including Teacher's College, Columbia University, New York University, University of Vermont, and New Jersey State Teacher's College. Ms. Stern is coauthor of the *Structural Reading Program, Gould-Stern Early Reading Activities, Children Discover Arithmetic,* and the *Structural Arithmetic Program.*

Toni S. Gould has been a reading consultant in New York City for over thirty-five years. She is author of *Reading–The Right Start* and co-author of the widely used *Structural Reading Program, Structural Arithmetic Program,* and *The Early Years of Childhood* and *Children Discover Reading.* Ms. Gould has taught at Bank Street College of Education, Hunter College, Lehman College, and has conducted workshops for teachers in schools and colleges throughout the United States.

Acknowledgements

The authors want to thank the friends and teachers who have offered so many suggestions and tried out workbook ages for us: Barbara Haney, The Spence School: Alison Lankenau, The Nightingale-Bamford School; Peggy Mabie and the staff of the Gateway School of New York City. Children who have given us good ideas for games are Alexandra Haney, Kate Slattery, and Heidi Simon. Our most special thanks go to our grandchildren Gabriela Gould-Porras and Philip Stern Brennan.

Copyright © 2007 Stern Math, LLC. All rights reserved. No part of this book may be reproduced or utilized in any form or by any electronic or mechanical means, including photocopying, without permission in writing from the publisher. Printed in U.S.A.
ISBN 0-9779132-2-8 (Previously ISBN 0-8388-7082-1)

Structural Arithmetic Materials

Set A

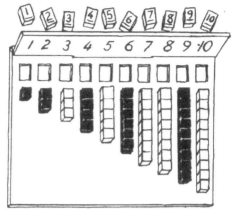

Counting board with number markers 1 to 10, number guide, and number blocks

Extra number markers and signs

10-box with number blocks

Number boxes 1 to 10

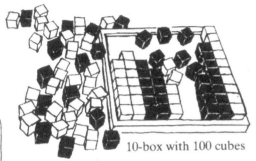

10-box with 100 cubes

Pattern boards 1 to 10

Set B

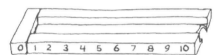 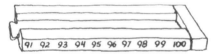

Number track 1 to 100

10-box

4-blocks

3-blocks

2-blocks

Unit cubes

Number blocks 1 to 9 (for multiplication and division)

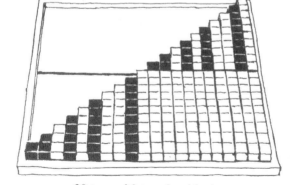

20-tray with number blocks

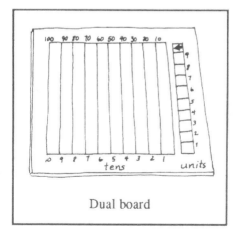

Dual board

Contents

Introduction	1
The Structural Arithmetic Program	2
Pretest for *Structural Arithmetic II*	5
Review of Basic Addition and Subtraction Facts	6
Unit 1. Addition and Subtraction	7
Unit 2. The Structure of Two-Place Numbers	14
Unit 3. Teen Numbers	18
Unit 4. Problem Solving	24
Unit 5. Two-Place Numbers in the Number Track	32
Unit 6. Switching from Ones to Tens	36
Unit 7. Adding and Subtracting Two-Place Numbers	42
Unit 8. Transfer to Higher Decades	51
Unit 9. Teen Facts	55
Unit 10. Telling Time	59
Unit 11. More Teen Facts	64
Unit 12. Sums of 11 and 12; Subtracting from 11 and 12	69
Unit 13. More Teen Facts	72
Unit 14. Regrouping in Addition and Subtraction	78
Unit 15. The Structure of Three-Place Numbers	84
Mastery Tests	87
Summary of Teen Facts in Addition	89
Summary of Teen Facts in Subtraction	90
100-Square	91

INTRODUCTION

Developing Cognitive Thinking

The goal of the Structural Arithmetic Program is to develop cognitive thinking and an appreciation for the exactness and clarity of mathematics. Arithmetic, a branch of mathematics, can and should be taught from the beginning so as to enable children to think and to reason things out for themselves.

Experiments with the materials form the core of the program. The materials, which are designed to make the structure of the number system visible, enable pupils to discover number concepts and to gain insight into the meaning of each operation: addition, subtraction, multiplication, and division.

Teaching Number Facts in Structurally Related Groups

Teaching number facts by rote and in isolation takes from children the joy of using their minds. Such an approach prevents pupils from developing the ability to think and to reason. Children who figure out an addition fact by counting beads or using rods learn it in isolation, thus missing an opportunity to reason. The Structural Arithmetic Program introduces facts in groups, giving children insight into the characteristic structures common to these facts. This procedure allows children to develop the ability to think mathematically as they figure out the relationships and express the generalization in their own words.

As an example, let us look at the fact $9 + 5 = 14$. Children discover all the combinations that result from adding ones to tens in the 20-tray: $10 + 1 = 11$, $10 + 2 = 12$, and so on. They then substitute a 9-block for the 10-block. By adding a number block such as 5 to the 9-block, they discover that the sum is 1 less than if they had added 5 to 10: $10 + 5$ is 15; $9 + 5$ is only 14. They apply this generalization to other numbers and reason that it holds true for all adding-to-9 facts. Thus, the fact has not been learned in isolation but in a context where its relationship to a whole group of facts can be seen and applied.

Developing Concepts by Measuring, Not by Counting

When children see an example such as $9 + 4 = \_\_$, they often respond by counting "10, 11, 12, 13." Teachers may assume that encouraging children to count will one day result in their stopping counting and saying, "13." In actuality, each time they see $+ 4$, they automatically count. For the counting child, 9 plus 4 does not equal 13; it makes 13 by counting. If children count the total incorrectly as 14, they have no way to check that result except by another uncertain counting procedure. On the other hand, in Structural Arithmetic, the two addends 9 and 4 actually measure 13 in the number track. This leaves an unforgettable picture in the children's minds. It becomes obvious, then, that counting is a rote procedure that stands in the way of children's learning to think or reason.

Developing Spatial Thinking

In Structural Arithmetic children add together two quantities and measure their total; for instance, the 10-block plus the 3-block measures 13. Working with materials in this way allows children to experiment with ideas and to figure out other relationships. They might take one of the blocks from the total and leave the other one, thus discovering the related subtraction facts, $13 - 3 = 10$ and $13 - 10 = 3$. Whether they are measuring with blocks or working with cubes, they are using spatial thinking to help them reason. Each experiment leaves a mental image that the children can turn around in their minds to explore new relationships.

Economy of Learning—The Result of Transfer

By making the structure of our number system visual, the Structural Arithmetic materials make it possible for children to transfer facts to other areas. If they know that $5 + 2 = 7$, they can discover that this fact holds true in any decade by measuring in the number track, $15 + 2 = 17$, $25 + 2 = 27$, or $65 + 2 = 67$. By working with cubes and 10-blocks in the dual board the children can find that what is true for ones is also true for tens, $50 + 20 = 70$. The result is an immense economy in the number of facts that have to be memorized.

The Structural Arithmetic Program is designed to help children develop number concepts and arrive at generalizations essential to the understanding of mathematics. To the degree in which they develop their ability to think with numbers, their work will be creative and fulfilling.

The Structural Arithmetic Program

Grade 1

Materials:
Set A (see inside front cover)
Experimenting with Numbers
Structural Arithmetic I (workbook)
Structural Arithmetic I Teacher's Guide and Answer Key

Sequential Development of Concepts

Children:
- discover addition and subtraction facts with sums of 10 and less
- learn to record these facts
- learn to solve for x
- master facts through understanding the characteristics of each structurally related group:
  combinations that make 10
  adding 0, adding to 0
  adding 1, adding to 1
  adding 2, adding to 2
  addition—doubles and neighbors
  difficult facts: $5 + 3, 3 + 5; 6 + 3, 3 + 6$
  combinations that make 1 through combinations that make 9
- related subtraction facts for each group (see charts on page 6)
- solve word problems using these facts

Grade 2 and Advanced Grade 1

Materials:
Set B (see inside front cover)
Structural Arithmetic II (workbook)
Structural Arithmetic II Teacher's Guide and Answer Key

Sequential Development of Concepts

Children:
- review facts learned in grade 1
- discover structure of 2-place numbers
- learn to analyze word problems
- learn the value of coins
- learn to tell time and write time
- master facts through understanding the characteristics of each structurally related group:
  adding 9, adding to 9
  adding 8, adding to 8
  combinations that make 11 and 12
  doubles and neighbors (teens)
  related subtraction facts for each group
- transfer facts to higher decades
- build 3-place numbers
- understand regrouping in addition and subtraction

Grade 3

Materials:
Set B (see inside front cover)
Structural Arithmetic III (workbook)
Structural Arithmetic III Teacher's Guide and Answer Key

Sequential Development of Concepts

Children:
- review 100 basic addition and subtraction facts
- review regrouping in addition and subtraction
- study 3-, 4-, and 5-place numbers
- discover and master the multiplication facts (tables 1 through 12)
- understand the relationship between multiplication and division
- master the basic division facts
- discover division with remainders
- understand the reasons underlying the steps in long division
- analyze problems systematically

Grade 4

Materials:
Set B (see inside front cover) and fraction materials
Structural Arithmetic IV (workbook)
Structural Arithmetic IV Teacher's Guide and Answer Key

Sequential Development of Concepts

Children:
- study the structure of numbers to 1,000,000
- learn to round off numbers
- study the structure of fractions
- use fraction materials to add, subtract, multiply, and divide fractions
- understand decimal notation
- learn to use decimals in addition, subtraction, multiplication, and division
- understand ratio and proportion
- understand and use percent
- solve problems using these concepts

Teaching in Small Groups

Learning by Insight

Children learn more effectively when they work together in small groups than when they work alone in workbooks. The Structural Arithmetic experiments and games can be carried out by the class as a whole; however, children will learn more if the class is divided into groups of six to ten children. In a small group everyone has more opportunities to handle the materials and to make their own discoveries. The following suggestion has proved successful in many classrooms. Groups A and B use the materials Monday, Wednesday, and Friday, while Group C works independently. On Tuesday and Thursday the groups switch, giving Group C two days of experimenting, while the others work independently. It is more productive for children to learn through insight and understanding several times a week than to spend five days a week in less meaningful drill.

Sustaining Attention and Thinking Ahead

These skills are important for every child, but above all for children with attention disorders. Playing a game full of interest heightens these children's excitement and helps them lengthen their span of attention. Once totally involved, they do not just give an answer and retire, but become curious about what the others are going to do. This encourages them to think ahead and plan what they will do when it is their turn.

Discovering Other Solutions

When children work in a group, they can watch someone else solve a problem in a way quite different from the one they would have used. Such experiences are important as they alert students to new ways of reasoning and of figuring things out for themselves.

Learning to Abide by Rules

Learning to follow rules is difficult for all children, yet they soon realize a game can be fair and fun only when there are rules that everyone respects. This allows them to relax and concentrate on the concepts and the mental computation necessary for playing the game.

Structuring Games

Group games must be more than interesting: they should be structured to protect pupils on different levels of competence. The rules must not allow those children who most need the practice to be eliminated first. When children realize that a winner's victory is due to chance and not to being smart, many of them take heart. They see that they can expect to win, and this expectation keeps them paying attention until the very end of the game.

Making Up Games

Teachers and children sometimes need more games than can be included here, and they want them to be fun. Many teachers find that they themselves are able to make up good games.

Making up variations of games is a most important aspect of working with the Structural Arithmetic material. Here are some suggestions.

Structure Must Form the Context. Children need a context within which to work. This context should be structured in such a way that they can see how a generalization applies. The generalization explains how each group of facts is related. For example, consider this generalization: Adding 1 to a number results in the next higher number. Children really understand what this means when they see the 1-cube climbing up each step of the stair. They call it "the climbing 1." The context is the stair of blocks from 1 to 10.

Determining How Moves Will Be Made. The moves that the players make can be determined by various means—cards with numbers on them, number markers (see inside front cover), dice to be tossed, a stop-and-go cube, or dominoes with equations on them. The players take turns choosing a facedown card or domino and making the moves necessary to win. A move might be to add as many units as the sum of the dice, to find the blocks stated in the equation, or to build that number with tens and ones. Students take turn after turn with an eagerness to win and no feeling of boredom. In some games, the child who answers the first question can be allowed to make up the next question. Children also enjoy taking turns playing the role of teacher during games.

Teachers who have invented new games will find their pupils caught up in their own enthusiasm to a degree that increases their ability to absorb what they are learning. They respond to their teachers' involvement in the games. Beyond that, being creative makes a teacher's work more fulfilling. For these reasons we encourage teachers to try out variations and games of their own invention.

Improving Receptive Language

Good comprehension of spoken language is important for all children. When words and phrases seem unfamiliar, they can be clarified by the teacher through concrete demonstrations with the materials. Teachers should simplify directions by breaking them into smaller steps. This also allows the teacher to monitor comprehension at each step and to diagnose children's troubles. Since children enjoy following directions given by their classmates, they listen attentively when children are given roles of leadership.

Improving Expressive Language

Children who learn to use the language of mathematics accurately are better able to understand and to solve written problems. When they take the role of teacher, an option for every game, they learn to express themselves clearly. In order to tell classmates what to do, they must have the number relationships clearly in mind. They might call on a friend and say, "I have hidden 19 in all. If I have 10 in one hand, what is in the other hand?" When the friend answers, "The 9-block," they know they have stated the problem accurately. The ability to use language well is an essential step in the development of mathematical reasoning.

Children with Learning Differences

Children with learning differences who learn mathematics with the Structural Arithmetic materials respond with great joy. Handling the materials allows them to carry out procedures with real objects. Thus, when they encounter procedures in writing, the words have meaning for them. For example, when children begin to add big numbers, they are told they must "regroup" and "carry one." These terms can baffle them. What happens if they experiment with the Structural Arithmetic materials first? If they add 6 cubes to 4 cubes in the dual board, they find that these ten cubes fill the ones compartment but that they cannot record this amount with a single digit. They hear that they must "regroup." To do this, they exchange 10 cubes for a solid 10-block, which they regroup by carrying it into the tens compartment. Now that they have physically "regrouped" the cubes, these children find it easy to visualize the procedure and record it on paper. Thus, the main areas of potential weakness are strengthened, for it is insufficient language skills and poor memories that cause these children to become frightened and humiliated when they try to learn mathematics by rote. Although children with learning differences find it almost impossible to understand numerical relationships through verbal explanations, teachers are seldom trained to present mathematical concepts in a comprehensible manner. The Structural Arithmetic approach, however, enables teachers to communicate mathematical ideas through experiments with materials rather than through words alone.

Teaching Remedial Students

Older students who have been failing in their work with number symbols may have no notion of the concepts that lie behind these symbols. They soon improve when they have an explanation they can see and feel and "hang on to." It is not difficult for the teacher to make the basic work appealing to older children. Many of these pupils have never had a foundation in mathematics. The tasks described for younger students can be set up for the older ones to practice in much the same way as they practice basic skills for sports. For example, students can compete with themselves by keeping a chart of the length of time it takes them to do adding-to-9 facts.

Attractive games for building basic concepts are described on pages 8 to 10. Children usually gain self-confidence from understanding previously incomprehensible problems and experience pleasure in finding that they can think. The result is an appreciation of the materials and a renewed respect for themselves.

How to Use the Lesson Plans

The materials of Set B form the core around which this cognitive approach is built. Children use the materials in games and experiments to develop new concepts; they do not write pages and pages of drilled number symbols but discover number relationships for themselves. The answers they give are the end products of their own thoughts, not something they have memorized.

The Teacher's Guide and Answer Key

Fifteen units present new ideas sequentially. An introduction at the beginning of each unit outlines and describes the concepts and clarifies the vocabulary.

A games and demonstrations page with illustrations and descriptions presents key games and demonstrations for lessons in that unit. The illustrations enable teachers to see at a glance which materials to use, how to present them, what questions to ask, and what answers to expect. Additional games are provided as part of each lesson. The notation *ExN* indicates that a game is illustrated or explained in greater detail in *Experimenting with Numbers.**

The purpose of each lesson is stated at the beginning. A section called group activity describes games and experiments with materials through which students will discover, explore, and then practice each new procedure. Remember that children often need several days to abstract new concepts from their concrete experiences; provide opportunities for practice at the chalkboard or on paper. Each lesson should contain some oral work as it is an important factor in building a good foundation for mental arithmetic.

The workbook should be used only after children have

---

*Margaret Stern, *Experimenting with Numbers* (Cambridge, Mass.: Educators Publishing Service, Inc., 1988).

nearly mastered the work of that lesson through using the materials, oral work, and some practice at the chalkboard. The workbook page enables teachers to evaluate whether students have learned the contents of the lesson; it is not intended for drill. Tests at the end of each unit enable teachers to determine if more work is necessary before going on to new concepts. Review games are suggested before each test as preparation for that test.

PRETEST FOR *STRUCTURAL ARITHMETIC II*

Before beginning Unit 1 determine which students have mastered the basic facts. An example of the combinations your pretest might cover is shown below. For students who need more work, play the games at the beginning of Unit 1 until they know these facts. Students who have mastered the facts can proceed directly to Lesson 1. Students who need extensive work should review *Structural Arithmetic I*.

```
                       SAMPLE PRETEST

        7      6      8      5          1      5      3      6
       +3     +2     +2     +3         +9     +4     +5     +4
       __     __     __     __         __     __     __     __


        4      2      4      2          2      3      5      2
       +5     +3     +4     +8         +5     +6     +5     +7
       __     __     __     __         __     __     __     __


        4      7      2     10          6      5      3      4
       +6     +2     +6     +0         +3     +2     +7     +3
       __     __     __     __         __     __     __     __


       10      9     10      9         10      8      9     10
       −0     −2     −8     −5         −2     −3     −6     −3
       __     __     __     __         __     __     __     __


        7      9      7     10          8      9     10      7
       −3     −4     −4     −6         −4     −7     −7     −5
       __     __     __     __         __     __     __     __


       10      7      9      8         10      9      8     10
       −5     −2     −3     −6         −4     −8     −5     −9
       __     __     __     __         __     __     __     __
```

REVIEW OF BASIC ADDITION AND SUBTRACTION FACTS

The following brief summaries outline how the basic addition and subtraction facts were taught in *Structural Arithmetic I*. Because the facts described in each group are structurally related, children can master them by understanding one generalization. For students who have not yet mastered these facts (see pretest), begin by playing the games in Unit 1.

Adding 0; Adding to 0. To pattern boards (or paper patterns) with cubes, add no cubes (zero); the pattern remains the same (1 + 0 = 1). Fill the 10-box with blocks; add the 10-block to an empty row (0 + 10 = 10).

Adding 1; Adding to 1. To the stair of blocks 1 to 10 add the 1-block to each step. Adding to a number results in the next higher number (1 + 1 = 2). The same holds true for adding a number to 1.

Adding 2; Adding to 2. Add the 2-block to each step of the stair. Adding 2 to an even number results in the next higher even number (2 + 2 = 4); adding 2 to an odd number results in the next higher odd number (3 + 2 = 5).

Combinations That Make 10. Fill the 10-box with blocks.

Doubles and Neighbors—Addition. Fill the pattern boards with cubes. The even numbers are doubles (2 + 2 = 4, 4 + 4 = 8). The odd numbers are sums of neighbors (3 + 2 = 5).

Difficult Combinations. 5 + 3 = 8; 6 + 3 = 9. See *Structural Arithmetic I Teacher's Guide*, p. 49.

Subtracting 0; Remainder of 0. Subtract no cubes from a pattern and the pattern remains (1 − 0 = 1). Take all cubes away and zero remains (4 − 4 = 0).

Subtracting 1; Remainder of 1. Fill the pattern boards with cubes. Subtracting 1 cube from each pattern yields the next lower pattern (10 − 1 = 9; 9 − 1 = 8, etc.). Subtract the next lower number from a pattern, and the remainder is 1 (10 − 9 = 1; 8 − 7 = 1; 7 − 6 = 1).

Subtracting 2; Remainder of 2. Subtracting 2 cubes from each even pattern results in the next lower even number (8 − 2 = 6). Subtracting 2 from each odd number yields the next lower odd number (7 − 2 = 5).

Subtracting from 10. From the combinations that make 10, subtract one block, and the other remains.

Doubles and Neighbors—Subtraction. Subtracting one addend from a double leaves the other (8 − 4 = 4). Subtracting one addend from a neighbor leaves the other (7 − 3 = 4; 9 − 4 = 5).

Difficult Combinations. 9 − 6 = 3; 8 − 5 = 3. See *Structural Arithmetic I Teacher's Guide*, p. 49.

UNIT 1. ADDITION AND SUBTRACTION

Lessons in this unit:
1. Solving for X
2. 10-Facts
3. Column Addition
4. Ordinal Numbers
5. Which One? How Many?

Reviewing the Basic Facts

Unit 1 reviews the 100 basic addition and subtraction facts covered in *Structural Arithmetic I* (see the charts on page 6). Performance on the pretest will alert teachers to the facts that need more time to be mastered. Games on page 10 offer more variations for children who need more practice.

Until children have thoroughly mastered the 100 basic addition and subtraction facts, they will be unable to move easily through the succeeding levels. For this reason, children should play the games in Unit 1 until they have mastered these facts.

Children New to Structural Arithmetic

It is important that children who begin the Structural Arithmetic program in second grade learn to identify the blocks and know the combinations with sums of 10 or less as well as the related subtraction facts.

Classrooms without Set A

If the classroom has Set B materials only (see inside front cover), the teacher must reassemble the blocks as follows. Remove blocks 1 to 10 from the 20-stair in the 20-tray and put them into one of the 10-boxes. Fill in the 10-box with blocks 1 to 9 from the 20-stair (see inside front cover). If more 10-boxes are needed for additional groups, they can be filled with blocks from the sets of blocks for multiplication. Number patterns can be built from single cubes in odd or even patterns on rectangles of paper (see inside front cover, pattern boards 1 to 10). Games that require Set A materials will specify "Set A" next to the title. Teachers who do not have Set A should adapt Set B materials as described in order to play these games.

GAMES AND DEMONSTRATIONS

Snake Game—Learning the Names of the Blocks
(Set A)

Materials: counting board with blocks and number guide in place, number markers 1 to 10, tray

- Explain the Snake Game: the team members take turns picking a number that tells them which block to get for their team's snake.
- Put number markers 1 to 10 facedown on a tray.
- Pass the tray of number markers to a child.
* Say, "Choose a number; put it back" (in the board). The child chooses 9 and puts it in the counting board.
- Say, "You can take that block for your snake."
- The child adds the 9-block to her team's snake.

Calling Back Game

Materials: same as above

- Leave the blocks scattered on the table.
- Place number markers facedown on a tray.
- Each child picks a number marker, reads it, finds the corresponding block, and returns both block and number marker to the counting board.

Hiding Game

Materials: 10-box, number blocks 1 to 10 and 1 to 9

Note: Children learn the combinations that make 10 by filling the 10-box with blocks.

- Scatter the blocks next to an empty 10-box.
- Say, "Close your eyes." (Hide a combination of blocks that make 10, one block in each hand.)
* Say, "Open your eyes. I have 10 altogether."
- Continue, "In one hand I have 8" (place it in the 10-box).
- Ask, "What is in the other hand?"
- When a child answers, "2," show the block.
- The child adds the 2-block to the 8 to make 10.

Scarf Game—Subtracting from 10

Materials: 10-box, number blocks 1 to 10, scarf

- Scatter the blocks next to the empty 10-box.
- Say, "Close your eyes." (Beneath a scarf hide two blocks that make 10, such as 8 and 2.)
- Say, "Open your eyes; under this scarf I have hidden two blocks that make 10."
- "If I take the 8 away (remove the 8-block), what is left?" (2). Remove the scarf to check.
- Call on a child to state the subtraction fact $10 - 8 = 2$. (*ExN*, p. 58)

*An asterisk indicates that this part of the experiment is illustrated.

GAMES AND DEMONSTRATIONS

Hidden Blocks—Word Problems in Subtraction
Materials: number blocks 1 to 10, number markers 1 to 10, 0, +, −, and =, tray, box

- Place the number blocks on the table.
- Put the number markers faceup in a tray.
- Explain that you will hide two blocks under a box and then tell a story about them. The children will record the story with the number markers.
- When the children's eyes are closed, hide blocks 9 and 1 under the box.
- Say, "Open your eyes."
* Say, "I had 10 bananas. I ate 1 of them" (withdraw the 1-cube from the box).
- Ask, "How many are left?" (9).
- Ask a child, "Would you record that story with numbers?"
- The child selects number markers and dictates to herself as she records, $10 - 1 = 9$.
- Have another child read the equation and lift up the box to show that the 9-block is left.
- Put the 1-block back with the 9-block to show the corresponding addition fact.
- Do other problems.

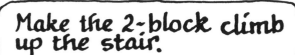

The Climbing 2—Adding 2 to a Number
Materials: 10-box, number blocks 1 to 10, extra 2-block

- Have the children build a stair in the 10-box.
- Demonstrate the climbing 2 by placing an extra 2-block on the first step.
- Elicit that "1 and 2 equal 3."
- The child who makes the next move says, "2 and 2 are 4."
* The next child puts the 2-block on 3.
- The child states, "3 and 2 equal 5."
- The block climbs the stair until the last fact: 8 and 2 are 10.

Building a Stair with a Step of 2
Materials: number blocks 1 to 10

- Scatter blocks 1 to 10 on the table.
- Ask a child to build a stair with a step of 2.
- It will be possible to build two different stairs.
- The child who starts with 2 builds 2, 4, 6, 8, 10.
- The child who starts with 1 builds 1, 3, 5, 7, 9.

GAMES AND DEMONSTRATIONS

Oral Review

Filling Boxes 1 to 9—Facts with Sums of 1 to 9
(Set A)
Materials: number boxes 1 to 9, number blocks 1 to 9 and 1 to 8

Children are excited to find they can play the games they learned using the 10-box by fitting blocks into boxes 1 to 9.* They should fill the boxes in order; the 1-box holds just the 1-block and gives one combination: $1 + 0 = 1$. In the 2-box they discover 2 combinations: $2 + 0 = 2$ and $1 + 1 = 2$. In the 3-box there are 3 combinations, and so forth. *Note:* The 6-box is a good box to concentrate on because 6, an even number, has a double ($3 + 3$) in the middle, just as 10 has the double $5 + 5$. In contrast, the odd number boxes 3, 5, 7, and 9 never have a double in the middle; they have pairs of neighbors.

Meshing Together Two Stairs—Facts That Make 10
Materials: 10-box, number blocks 1 to 10 and 1 to 9

Ask a child to build a stair by carefully standing blocks 1 to 10 on end along the bottom edge of a 10-box. On the opposite side build a vertical stair from 9 to 1. Begin by pushing the 9-block down. Ask a child, "9 needs . . . ?" The child pushes down the 1-block in his stair and answers, "1." Continue by pushing down 8. Say, "8 needs . . . ?" A child says, "2," and pushes it down. (*ExN*, p. 36)

Which Blocks Are Missing?—Facts That Make 10
Materials: 10-box, number blocks 1 to 10 and 1 to 9

The children place combinations of blocks in sequence in the 10-box: $1 + 9, 2 + 8, 3 + 7 \ldots 10 + 0$. Say, "Close your eyes." Hide one combination of blocks ($5 + 5$). Say, "Open your eyes! Which blocks are missing?" Call on a child to answer and put the blocks back in the box. (*ExN*, p. 37)

What Comes Next?—Facts with Sums of 1 to 10
Materials: 10-box, number blocks 1 to 10 and 1 to 9, cardboard cover

The children fill the 10-box as above. Cover the filled box with a piece of cardboard. Ask, "What comes first? 1 and what?" After a child answers, move the cover to check the answer. Ask, "What comes next?" Help the children figure out each combination. They should name each successive combination. (*ExN*, p. 37)

Subtraction Facts
Once the children know the addition facts, they can figure out the subtraction facts. Playing the Scarf Game is a good review (see p. 8).

Written Review

Sticker Game—+2, −2 Facts; Doubles and Neighbors
Materials: 10-box, index cards with $+2$, -2 facts and doubles and neighbors facts

Build the stair from 1 to 10 in the 10-box. Say, "Close your eyes." Hide a folded sticker beneath a block, perhaps 5. Show the card that tells where the sticker is: $7 - 2 = \_\_$. The player who reads the example looks under the 5-block for the sticker. Work with one group of related facts at a time, either the $+2$ or -2 facts or doubles and neighbors.

Missing Addends—Facts with Sums 1 to 10
Materials: 10-box, number blocks 1 to 10 and 1 to 9, number markers 1 to 10, index cards with addition facts ($9 + \_\_ = 10$, $8 + \_\_ = 10$, etc.), tray

Scatter the number blocks next to a 10-box. Turn the deck of cards facedown. Place the number markers faceup on a tray. A child picks a card ($3 + \_\_ = 10$), selects the correct combination of blocks, places number marker 7 on the equation, reads it, and keeps both card and blocks for the next game. (*ExN*, p. 56)

Problem Solving—Facts with Sums of 10
Materials: number blocks and cards from previous game

Each child has an equation with blocks from the last game. State a problem: "Chris had 4 marbles and won 6 more. How many did Chris have then?" The child with the equation reads it and answers, "10 marbles."

Building Speed

Big Kids, Little Kids Game
Materials: 20-tray, number markers 1 to 10, extra 5-marker

Explain that number markers 0, 1, 2, 3, 4, and 5 represent little kids of those ages and put them in random order in the bottom section of the 20-tray. In the upper part place number markers 5, 6, 7, 8, 9, and 10 and call these the big kids. Explain that each big kid must pick up a little kid as fast as possible—the 10-year-old picks up the baby of 0 age, 9 picks up the 1-year-old and so on—until each big kid has picked up a little kid. The point is to do this as quickly as possible. Each child has a turn matching up the big kids and little kids. The markers can be placed one above the other in a corner of the 20-tray.

Note: This popular game should be done only with children who have already mastered the combinations through using the materials. It forces students who are slow to focus in and work quickly; it should not be used as drill. Use the pattern boards to show children who mismatch 7 and 3 or 6 and 4 that the two odd numbers $7 + 3$ fit together as do the two even numbers $6 + 4$.

---

*These combinations of blocks can be arranged side by side without the boxes.

REVIEW GAMES FOR LESSON 1

Doubles and Neighbors in the Counting Board (Set A)
Materials: counting board, number markers 1 to 10, two sets of blocks 1 to 5
Doubles
- Children take turns selecting and putting before them two like blocks: 1, 1; 2, 2; 3, 3; 4, 4; 5, 5.
- Put the marker for 10 above the 10-groove.
- Say, "I want two blocks the same that make 10."
- A child puts two 5-blocks in the 10-groove.
- Children fill the even grooves 2, 4, 6, and 8 in the same way and learn that these are called "the doubles."

Neighbors
- Leave the blocks for the doubles in place.
- From the double 5 + 5 remove a 5-block and put it in the 9-groove.
- Ask, "What does 5 need to make 9?" (Take the 4-block from the double 4 + 4 and add it to the 5-block.)
- Elicit, "5 needs 4 to make 9."
- Explain that we call 5 and 4 "neighbors."
- Fill the groove for each odd number with consecutive blocks (neighbors), 4 + 3, 3 + 2, 2 + 1, and 1 + 0, in the same way.

Subtracting 2 from Even Numbers
Materials: 10-box, number blocks 1 to 10, toy cat, cardboard screen
- Build the even stair in the 10-box: 2, 4, 6, 8, 10.
- Elicit that there is a step of 2 between the blocks.
- Say, "Put in the block 2 smaller than 10."
- A child places the 8-block before the 10-block.
- On the board write 10 − 2 = 8.
- Continue until the stair has been completed.

Where Is the Cat?
- On the table stand on end a stair of even number blocks.
- Place a screen in front of it.
- Put a toy cat on one step, perhaps 6.
- Say, "The cat is on the block 2 less than 8. Where is the cat?"
- Call on a child to name the block (6).
- Move the screen so the children can see the cat.
- This child becomes the teacher for the next turn.

Subtracting 2 from Odd Numbers
- Have a child build the stair of odd number blocks: 1, 3, 5, 7, 9.
- Play Where Is the Cat?, placing the cat on an odd number block and giving the example orally.

LESSON 1. Solving for X

Purpose: To introduce the concept of solving for X. To review the facts from the groups doubles and neighbors and subtracting 2 and 3 from numbers.

Group Activity
Materials: number blocks 1 to 10, index card labeled X

Doubles and Neighbors
- Use the index card to hide a block.
- Say, "Close your eyes." Hide the 5-block.
- Say, "Open your eyes. We call the mystery block X. X equals 3 + 2." Set the blocks beside the card.
- On the chalkboard write $X = 3 + 2$.
- A child says, "X is 5," removes the card to reveal the 5-block, and writes on the board, $X = 5$.

Subtracting 2
- Build the stair of even numbers: 2, 4, 6, 8, 10.
- Set aside two consecutive even blocks such as 8 and 10.
- Hide the 8-block with the card.
- On the board write $X = 10 − 2$.
- A child reads the equation, says "8," removes the card, and writes $X = 8$ on the chalkboard.

Workbook Page: **A** and **B**. Go over the facts orally. The children finish the page independently.

SOLVING FOR X

A

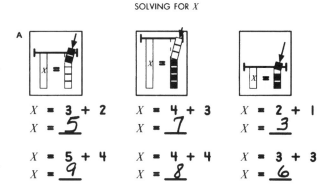

$X = 3 + 2$ $X = 4 + 3$ $X = 2 + 1$
$X = 5$ $X = 7$ $X = 3$

$X = 5 + 4$ $X = 4 + 4$ $X = 3 + 3$
$X = 9$ $X = 8$ $X = 6$

B

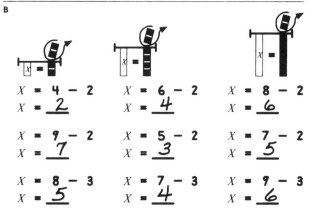

$X = 4 − 2$ $X = 6 − 2$ $X = 8 − 2$
$X = 2$ $X = 4$ $X = 6$

$X = 9 − 2$ $X = 5 − 2$ $X = 7 − 2$
$X = 7$ $X = 3$ $X = 5$

$X = 8 − 3$ $X = 7 − 3$ $X = 9 − 3$
$X = 5$ $X = 4$ $X = 6$

LESSON 2. 10-Facts

Purpose: To review the 10-facts in addition and subtraction.
Note: Children should master these basic facts before doing more advanced work.

Group Activity
Materials: strip of paper the size of a 10-block for each child, index cards with addition facts (8 + __ = 10), number blocks 1 to 9

The Paper-10 Game
- Children draw a card, read the equation, and ask you for the blocks, "I need 8 and 2."
- Each child places the blocks on his or her paper strip.
- They keep the filled strips for the next game.

Subtracting from 10
- Each child has two blocks on a paper strip.
- Call on the children to demonstrate a subtraction fact with their blocks and state the equation, for example, "10 minus 2 leaves 8."

Workbook Page: Go over the page orally. Play other games if needed. The children finish the page independently.

8 + 2 = 10	10 − 2 = 8
2 + 8 = 10	10 − 8 = 2
7 + 3 = 10	10 − 7 = 3
3 + 7 = 10	10 − 3 = 7
6 + 4 = 10	10 − 6 = 4
4 + 6 = 10	10 − 4 = 6
9 + 1 = 10	10 − 9 = 1
1 + 9 = 10	10 − 1 = 9
5 + 5 = 10	10 − 5 = 5

LESSON 3. Column Addition

Purpose: To study how to add more than two numbers.
Group Activity
Materials: 10-box filled with blocks
- On the chalkboard write 3 + 3 + 2 = __ .
- A child places these blocks end to end.
- Explain that we can add only two numbers at a time.
- Elicit that 3 and 3 are 6; replace the 3-blocks with one 6-block.
- Elicit that it is easy to add 6 + 2.
- On the chalkboard write other numbers to be added in column form.
- Children should learn to keep the sum of the first pair of numbers in their heads and add the third number to it.

Hiding Game
Materials: 10-box filled with blocks
- Hide three blocks behind your back (3, 5, 2).
- Say, "I have three blocks that make 10 in all; in one hand I have 3 + 5. What is in the other hand?"

Workbook Page: A and **B**. Go over the demonstration examples and problem. The children finish the page independently.

COLUMN ADDITION

A (2+3)+ 4 = ?
5 + 4 = 9

2
3 } 5
+4
9

3	5	1	6	7	4
2	3	5	2	0	3
+3	+2	+3	+2	+2	+2
8	10	9	10	9	9

5	4	2	5	2	6
1	1	1	1	2	3
+3	+4	+6	+2	+5	+0
9	9	9	8	9	9

B Ann won **2** red marbles,
3 green marbles,
and **3** yellow marbles.
How many marbles
did she win?

2
3
+3
8

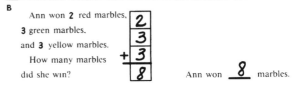

Ann won __8__ marbles.

LESSON 4. Ordinal Numbers

Purpose: To learn that numbers can also tell the order that one item comes in.

Note: In arithmetic a number such as 3 or 4 stands for a collection of units; this is the quantitative, or cardinal, sense. When number 4 appears on a house or the page of a book, it means just one house or one page in a certain order.

Group Activity

Materials: 10 index cards labeled with numbers 1 to 10
- Seat the children in a row and pass out the numbered cards in sequence.
- Ask, "Who is first?" Write *first* and *1st* on the chalkboard, emphasizing the *st*.
- The child with 2 is second. Write *second* and *2nd* and point out the *nd*.
- Introduce *third* in the same way and then go from *fourth* to *tenth*.
- Give oral directions to the children: The sixth child should stand up. The first child should turn around.

Workbook Page: Explain that the picture shows a department store with something different on each floor. The children write in the numbers from 1st to 10th and then finish the page independently.

ORDINAL NUMBERS

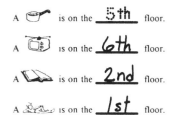

A 🥘 is on the **5th** floor.

A 📺 is on the **6th** floor.

A 📖 is on the **2nd** floor.

A 🐊 is on the **1st** floor.

Hats are on the **7**th floor.

LESSON 5. Which One? How Many?

Purpose: To study both the cardinal and ordinal use of numbers.

Group Activity

Materials: 10 different-colored cubes (or toy cars or animals), number markers 1 to 10
- Place the 10 items in a row and label each with a number marker from 1 to 10.
- Say to a child, "Give me car number 5."
- Elicit that this is just one car, but it comes at the *fifth* place in the row.
- Now say, "Give me 5 cars."
- Elicit that 5 now means a group of 5 cars.
- Give other children a chance to give you a group of cars (cubes or animals) or just one car from a certain place.

Workbook Page: Elicit that on the left the question asks about which child has a hat, while on the right the question asks how many children there are. Go over the page orally. The children finish the page independently.

WHICH ONE? HOW MANY?

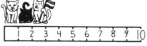

Which child has a hat?   How many children?
The **4th** child.   **4** children.

Which cat has a flag?   How many cats?
The **3rd** cat.   **3** cats.

Draw a line around **4** cats.

Draw a line around the **4**th cat.

Write an *X* on the **3**rd block.

Write an *X* on all **3** blocks.

UNIT 2. THE STRUCTURE OF TWO-PLACE NUMBERS

Lessons in this unit:
6. Working with Tens in the Dual Board
7. Switching from Ones to Tens
8. Reading and Writing Two-Place Numbers
9. Test

The Dual Board, 10-Blocks, and Cubes

When children look at a number such as 23 for the first time, they see two symbols that look quite similar in size. However, they soon learn that the number 23 represents a much bigger amount than the symbols 2 and 3 would seem to indicate. The new concept to be discovered lies in the arrangement of the written symbols. Although a knife and a fork is the same thing as a fork and a knife, children have to learn that this is not true for number symbols; 23 is not the same as 32. They will need many experiences with the materials before they understand the difference between 23 and 32.

By using the dual board children gain insight into the role that the position of each numeral plays. This is called positional notation. Children learn about the importance of position by building numbers in the dual board with the 10-blocks and the cubes. They then record the number with number markers or number symbols.

The dual board is designed to show the meaning behind each digit in a 2-place number. The compartment on the left is big and holds tens; the compartment on the right holds cubes, or ones.* The sizes of the two compartments guide the children so that in building a number they always put tens and ones in their correct places. They then label each amount with the relevant number marker. In a number such as 23, the number marker for 2 is placed below the tens, whereas 3 is placed below the ones. When the digits 23 are in place, the children can see for themselves the size that each digit stands for in the number 23—2 designates tens; 3 designates ones.

Mechanical work with the abacus is again being done in classrooms. Yet the counters of an abacus give children no more understanding of the actual amounts than do Arabic numerals. In either case students must memorize a rule they cannot verify: 10 ones have to be exchanged for 1 ten. One look at an abacus shows that the 10 counters in the ones row do not equal in size the single counter in the tens row. In the same fashion, the equivalence between 10 pennies and 1 dime cannot be seen. Children can never *discover* such relationships directly from the counters or coins, but must learn them by rote from other people.

We must understand that children gain *insight* into computation with numbers beyond 10 when they can see for themselves that 10 units of one denomination equal in size 1 unit of the next higher denomination. They come to realize that the familiar 10-block has a new role to play. The 10-block is so important because 10 is the base of our number system. When we record any amount we use a place value system, or positional notation. This simply means that the numeral to the left in a 2-digit number stands for a number of tens, while the numeral on the right stands for ones. In carrying out the experiments in Unit 2, children will discover they can deal with tens in the same way as they dealt with ones. They know that 2 and 2 make 4; now they apply this to tens—2 tens and 2 tens make 4 tens.

---

*On the dual board the printed names are *tens* and *units*. Since many teachers like the term *ones*, we decided to use *tens* and *ones* in this book. Both *units* and *ones* are correct.

GAMES AND DEMONSTRATIONS

Estimating Game (use with Lesson 6)
Materials: ~60 cubes, five 10-blocks
- Throw more than 50 cubes on the table (perhaps 54). The scattered cubes give the impression of a lot.
- Immediately cover the cubes and ask several children to give estimates of the total number.
- Lift the cover and, using a 10-block as a measure, form rows of 10 cubes. Group the leftover cubes to the right.
- The children can now see at a glance that the total is 5 rows of ten and 4 single cubes, or 54.

Note: The structure is so clear-cut that the number of cubes could never be thought to be 56 or 45. The 10-block can be handled as one piece and is superior to 1 dime or 1 counter on an abacus because it is marked in 10 units and actually equals 10 ones.

GAMES AND DEMONSTRATIONS

Store Game (use with Lesson 7)
Note: Tape a U-shaped frame on the dual board below the ones groove and the groove for the first ten (see illustrations). It should be large enough to hold two number markers side by side to record the 2-place number.
Materials: dual board, number markers 1 to 9 and 0, 10 cubes, number blocks

- Select one child to be storekeeper for the ones and another to be storekeeper for the tens.
- Display the dual board and number markers.
* Now hold number marker 3 below the ones compartment.
- Say, "Look where the number is. Whose store do I want something from?"
- The child with cubes says, "My store! 3 ones," and puts them into the ones compartment. (Remove the blocks after each turn.)
- Hold number 3 below the tens compartment; the storekeeper for tens puts 3 tens in place.
- Continue giving orders for ones or tens.
- Write 6 on the chalkboard; say, "I want 6 tens. How can I show that?" Write 0 next to 6 (60).
- In the dual board place the marker for 6 below the tens compartment and 0 below the ones compartment. Thus the children see that 60 means 6 tens, 0 ones.
- Explain that 0 is a place holder; it tells us that 6 belongs in the tens place.

Hiding Game (use with Lesson 8)
Note: Before playing the Hiding Game, have the children build a few 2-place numbers with the blocks and record them by placing a number marker below each compartment. Children may want to verify the total by counting all the units.
Materials: dual board, cubes, 10-blocks, number markers 1 to 9 and 0

- While the children's eyes are closed, hide several 10-blocks in one hand (perhaps 4) and a few cubes in the other (perhaps 6).
* Say, "Open your eyes. I have 46 altogether. In one hand I have 6 cubes" (place them in the ones compartment).
- Ask, "What is in the other hand?"
- A child answers, "4 tens!" and places the 10-blocks in the tens compartment.
- Let children take the role of teacher.

Note: For some children it helps to state the number by using two different tones of voice, "FORTY-six." This helps them hear the two different denominations separately.

LESSON 6. Working with Tens in the Dual Board

Purpose: To discover the role of ten in the number system, to name numbers of tens, and to add and subtract tens.
Group Activity
Estimating Game (see p. 14)
Working with Tens
Materials: dual board, cubes, 10-blocks

- Use the dual board to add and subtract different amounts of tens.
- For example, put 4 tens in each hand.
- Ask, "4 tens (put them in the board) and 4 more tens are how many tens?" (put them in to show the sum).
- Demonstrate easy subtraction facts as well.
- Call on a child to demonstrate this fact: 3 tens minus 1 ten leaves 2 tens.
- Write names for tens on the chalkboard and have children demonstrate the amount: Two tens are called twenty, three tens thirty, and so on. Explain that the ending *ty* means tens.

Workbook Page: The children finish the page independently.

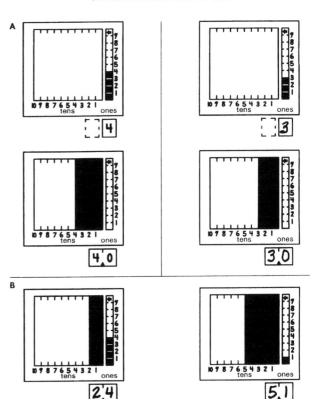

WORKING WITH TENS IN THE DUAL BOARD

LESSON 7. Switching from Ones to Tens

Purpose: To discover that a numeral in ones place stands for ones, while the same numeral in tens place stands for tens; to use zero as a place holder.
Group Activity
Store Game (see p. 15)
Note: Carefully follow the steps that help you introduce zero as a place holder.
Understanding the Concept of Place Value
Materials: dual board, cubes, 10-blocks, number markers 1 to 9 and 0

- Place a number marker such as 2 below the tens compartment and ask a child to put in 2 tens.
- Place the number marker for 0 beneath the ones compartment and elicit that this means no ones. Have a child name the number: "Twenty."
- Replace the 0 with a number such as 4 and have a child put in 4 ones.
- Guide the children in building other 2-place numbers such as 59, 43, and 31.
- Next, do the task in the opposite order; build 2-place numbers with blocks and have the children record them with numbers and read them.

Workbook Page: A. Go over the illustrations of the dual board.
The children finish the page independently.

LESSON 8. Reading and Writing Two-Place Numbers

Purpose: To study the structure of 2-place numbers; to learn to read their names.
Group Activity
Hiding Game (see p. 15)
Note: It is important for children to understand 2-place numbers when they hear them spoken, as they will hear these number names often in daily life.
Hiding Game Variation—Recording and Naming Numbers
- After each turn in the Hiding Game leave the blocks for the 2-place number in the dual board, such as 4 tens and 6 ones.
- Ask a child to record the number with markers (46).
- Call on another child to write the number name on the chalkboard (forty-six).
- Give different children a chance to be the leader in this game.

Workbook Page: Go over the first example. The children finish the page independently.

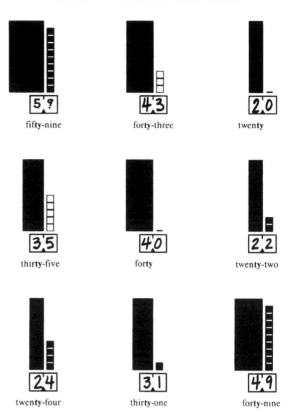

LESSON 9. Test

Purpose: To test knowledge of the number names for 2-place numbers and their composition.
Group Activity
Materials: dual board, cubes, 10-blocks
- Review the structure of 2-place numbers as follows: Place 3 tens and 5 ones in the dual board. Ask a child to record it with numbers and to write the name on the chalkboard (thirty-five).

Lotto Game
Materials: dual board, cubes, 10-blocks, lotto cards
Make two sets of lotto cards as shown.

12	63	82
54	Free	17
71	16	36

41	19	28
91	Free	60
45	14	21

- Give each child 9 cubes and a copy of either version of the lotto card.
- In the dual board, build a number with blocks that corresponds to a number on a lotto card.
- The children who have the number put a cube on it.
- Children with all spaces covered are the winners.

Workbook Page: Go over the first example. The children finish the page independently.

UNIT 3. TEEN NUMBERS

Lessons in this unit:
10. The 20-Stair
11. Teen Numbers
12. Breaking Teen Numbers into Tens and Ones
13. Pennies and Dimes
14. Pennies, Nickels, and Dimes
15. Pennies, Nickels, and Dimes
16. Test

The Teen Numbers

The numbers above 10 and up to 19 have the same structure; they are composed of 1 ten and a number of units, or ones. The names of these numbers, thirteen through nineteen, all end in *teen*. Thus they are called teen numbers. Although eleven and twelve also have the same structure, their names do not indicate this. We have extended the name *teen numbers* to include eleven and twelve as well.

The Stair from 1 to 20

Children will use the 20-tray to build the familiar part of the stair with blocks 1 to 10. At this point they discover they must piece together each of the next numbers using 1 ten and a number block (1 ten and 1 one, 1 ten and 1 two, and so on). Children are pleased to see that the stair 1 to 10 repeats itself on a base of 10.

Naming and Recording Teen Numbers

In Unit 2 the children learned to build and record 2-place numbers from 20 to 99. These symbols are easy for children to write correctly; they simply listen to the spoken name, such as "seventy-three," and write the numerals in the order they hear them, 73.

Children must learn that they cannot use this system to record teen numbers. If they do, they usually reverse the order of the digits and write *fourteen* as *41*. It is important to prevent this from happening in the first place. Before they write the numbers, children build each teen number in the dual board with 1 ten and a number of ones (or a number block) and record it with the number markers. Later, when they write the digits, they will do so by visualizing the structure of the teen number. When they hear "fourteen," they know it is 1 ten and 4 ones and write it correctly, 14.

It is this characteristic that makes the teen numbers stand out from the rest of the 2-place numbers and gives us the reason to study them as a special group of facts.

Breaking Teen Numbers into Tens and Ones

Children must gain the ability to separate teen numbers into 1 ten and a certain number of ones (16 = 10 and 6). Children should understand this basic concept before they study regrouping. Let us consider column addition:

$$\begin{array}{r} 16 \\ +37 \\ \hline \end{array}$$

We add ones to ones, 6 + 7 = 13; children must separate the component parts, getting 1 ten and 3 ones. They regroup them, saying something like, "Put down 3 and carry 1 ten to the tens column."

Money and the Teen Numbers

The dimes are the tens of our monetary system and the pennies are the ones. This enables children to understand that an amount expressed in cents, for example, 38¢, can be paid for by 3 dimes and 8 pennies.

The relationship between 1 dime and 2 nickels at first seems unreasonable to children, who think because the nickel is larger, it should be worth more than the dime. When these coins (or pictures of coins) are pasted on their corresponding blocks, children can see the relationship immediately. Since pictures of coins often look distorted to children, it is a good idea to use real coins. Children who may have problems can be helped to distinguish between coins by having the difference in texture, weight, and color pointed out to them. One ingenious teacher had children make pencil rubbings of coins to bring out the pictures pressed onto the surfaces of the coins. Lessons 13 to 15 include interesting games to help children become familiar with coins.

GAMES AND DEMONSTRATIONS

Building the 20-Stair (use with Lesson 10)
Materials: 20-tray, eleven 10-blocks, two sets of number blocks 1 to 9

- Children build the stair from 1 to 10 and stop.
* Say, "Think! Can you figure out how to build the next step?"
- Continue, "You need to piece each number together using a 10-block and a number block."
- A child puts in one 10-block and a cube as the next step and says, "10 and 1."
- A child builds the next step and says, "10 and 2."
- When the last step has been built, elicit that the stair "on top" is the same as the stair at the beginning, but one flight up.

Naming the Numbers 11 to 20 (use with Lesson 10)
Materials: same as above

- With your finger climb the stair from 1 to 20 as the children say each name in unison.
- Say, "Show me 4" (a child touches the 4-block). "Give me 14." (They must realize that 14 is 1 ten and 4 ones.)
- Continue until all these relationships have been identified (1 with 11, 2 with 12, and so on).

Recording Teen Numbers (use with Lesson 10)
Materials: dual board, 10-blocks, number blocks 1 to 9, number markers 1 to 9 and 0

- Place one 10-block in the tens compartment.
- A child places the number marker for 1 below the 10 block, and 0 below the empty ones compartment.
- Say, "I will build eleven." Add 1 cube to the ones compartment; change the markers to 11. (Empty the dual board after each turn.)
* Call on a child and say, "Build twelve. How many tens are there?"
- The child puts the marker for 1 under the 10-block and the marker for 2 under the 2-block.
- The children build the rest of the teen numbers from 11 to 20.

Snake Game (use with Lesson 11)
Materials: two sets of index cards with teen numbers, 10-blocks, number blocks 1 to 9

- Divide the class into two teams; each team will build a snake of blocks.
- Players alternate turning up a card, naming it, and putting the blocks on their team's snake.
- The team with the longer snake of blocks wins.

LESSON 10. The 20-Stair

Purpose: To discover the structure of the teen numbers; to learn their names and how to record them with symbols.

Group Activity

Building the 20-Stair and Naming the Numbers 11 to 20
(see p. 19)

Note: Children discover the structure of the teen numbers by building the 20-stair in the 20-tray.

Recording Teen Numbers (see p. 19)

Note: Help the children build each number in the dual board and learn to read each number name written on the chalkboard.

Hiding Game

Materials: 20-tray, eleven 10-blocks, two sets of number blocks 1 to 9

- Have the children build the stair from 1 to 20.
- When their eyes are closed, hide a teen number such as 16 behind your back (10 in one hand, 6 in the other).
- Say, "Open your eyes. I have hidden 16. In one hand is 10" (put it back in the stair).
- Ask, "What is in the other hand?"
- A child answers, "6," puts the 6-block back and states, "10 + 6 = 16."
- Call on different children to take the role of teacher.

Workbook Page
- Go over the illustration and the first example.
- Go over the words for numbers.
- The children finish the page independently.

THE 20-STAIR

eleven 11 = 1 ten 1 one
twelve 12 = 1 ten 2 ones
sixteen 16 = 1 ten 6 ones
nineteen 19 = 1 ten 9 ones
twenty 20 = 2 tens 0 ones

LESSON 11. Teen Numbers

Purpose: To construct each teen number, record it with symbols, and read its number name.

Group Activity

Snake Game (see p. 19)

Materials: Give the following to each of three groups: A) dual board, two 10-blocks, and number blocks 1 to 9; B) 20-tray, two 10-blocks, and number blocks 1 to 9; C) pencil and paper

- On the chalkboard write a number name, perhaps thirteen.
- Call on a child to read the name aloud.
- Group A builds 13 in the dual board, group B builds 13 in the 20-tray, and group C writes the number 13 on the papers.

Hiding Game

Materials: 20-tray, 10-blocks, 2 sets of number blocks 1 to 9

- The children build the stair from 1 to 20 in the 20-tray.
- When their eyes are closed, remove a teen number.
- Say, "Open your eyes. What number is missing?"
- The child who states the number has the next turn to hide a teen number.

Workbook Page: Go over the first example. The children finish the page independently.

TEEN NUMBERS

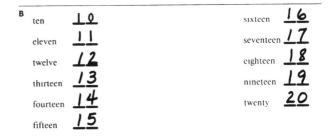

B
ten 10   sixteen 16
eleven 11   seventeen 17
twelve 12   eighteen 18
thirteen 13   nineteen 19
fourteen 14   twenty 20
fifteen 15

LESSON 12. Breaking Teen Numbers into Tens and Ones

Purpose: To break each teen number, by addition or subtraction, into ten and the appropriate number of ones.

Group Activity

Materials: number track, number blocks 1 to 9, two 10-blocks
- Ask a child to lay a pencil across the track at 18.
- Have a child build 18 with blocks 10 and 8 and record this as an addition fact, 10 + 8 = 18.

Dice Game

Materials: a cube with a plus sign on 3 sides and a minus sign on the other 3 sides, 9 index cards with a teen number on each card
- On the chalkboard write two headings:
    Addition   Subtraction
- A player selects a card (18), and tosses the die.
- If the minus sign is on top, he writes an equation in the subtraction column (18 − 8 = 10).
- If the plus sign is on top, he writes an equation in the addition column (10 + 8 = 18).

Workbook Page: **A.** Go over the illustration.
B. and **C.** The children finish the page independently.

BREAKING TEEN NUMBERS INTO TENS AND ONES

A
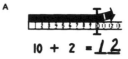 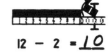

10 + 2 = _12_   12 − 2 = _10_

B

10 + 4 = _14_   14 − 4 = _10_

10 + 8 = _18_   18 − 8 = _10_

10 + 5 = _15_   15 − 5 = _10_

10 + 7 = _17_   17 − 7 = _10_

C
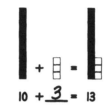

10 + _3_ = 13   13 − _3_ = 10

10 + _9_ = 19   19 − _9_ = 10

LESSON 13. Pennies and Dimes

Purpose: To work with dimes and pennies and relate these coins to the tens and ones of our number system.

Note: The value of a coin cannot be discovered by looking at its size. To prevent confusion, tape coins or pictures of coins on the blocks. Paste one penny on each of twenty 1-cubes and one dime on each of eleven 10-blocks.

Group Activity

Materials: blocks with coins, number track 1 to 20
- Have children show that 10 pennies equal 1 dime.
- Call on children to show different teen numbers built from 1 dime and several pennies.

Coin Game

Materials: blocks with coins, ten cards with a number from 10 to 20 on each
- Have a child select a card (13), build the amount with coins (on blocks), and name the total value, "13¢."
- Children keep their blocks with coins.
- Call the blocks back by name, "Calling back thirteen cents."

Workbook Page: Go over the illustrations and the two problems. The children finish the page independently.

PENNIES AND DIMES

A
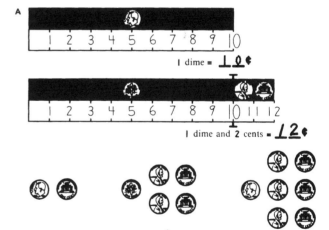

_11_¢   _14_¢   _16_¢

B
Jane had 10¢.
Her sister had 5¢.
How much money did they have together?

| 10 | + | 5 | = | 15 |

They had _15_¢

Bill had 17¢.
He used 7¢ to buy a ball.
He put the rest of the money in his bank.
How much money did Bill put in his bank?

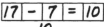

Bill put _10_¢ in his bank.

21

LESSON 14. Pennies, Nickels, and Dimes

Purpose: To work with pennies, nickels, and dimes.
Note: Paste a nickel on each of four 5-blocks. Use the twenty cubes and three of the 10-blocks prepared for Lesson 13.

Group Activity
Materials: number track 1 to 20, blocks with coins, pencil
- Place a pencil across the track at 10.
- Ask a child to put in a coin (block) worth 10¢.
- Ask for other ways to make 10¢ (2 nickels).
- A child places 2 nickels (blocks) on top of the dime.
- Have a child build 15¢ (3 nickels; 1 dime and 1 nickel).
- Make 16¢, 17¢, 18¢, and 19¢ by adding pennies to a dime and a nickel.

Mystery Coins
Materials: blocks with coins, box
- When children's eyes are closed, hide under a box blocks with coins totaling 20¢ or less.
- Say, "Open your eyes. The coins under this box are worth 13¢." (Some children may need to see 13¢ written on a card.)
- Children make 13¢ with different coins (1 dime and 3 pennies; 2 nickels and 3 pennies; 13 pennies).
- Lift up the box to see who guessed correctly.

Workbook Page: The children finish the page independently.

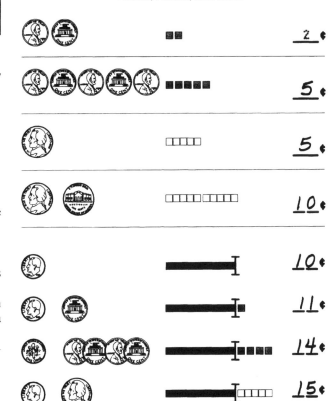

LESSON 15. Pennies, Nickels, and Dimes

Purpose: To work with small numbers of coins using pennies, nickels, and dimes.

Group Activity
Note: Dimes and *cents* correspond to the tens and ones of our number system. Children will work with amounts between 20¢ and 99¢.
Materials: ten 10-blocks with dimes, ten cubes with pennies
- Write amounts of money on the chalkboard to be demonstrated with 10-blocks such as 40¢, 60¢, and 80¢.
- Children show this with the blocks as 4 dimes, 6 dimes, and 8 dimes.
- Ask children to show 63¢ or 52¢ using blocks with dimes and blocks with pennies.

Playing Bank
Materials: 20 dimes, 10 nickels, and 10 pennies sorted into three different dishes, index cards on which you have written different amounts of money such as 64¢, 56¢, 32¢, 45¢, 15¢, 17¢
- Select a banker to be in charge of the coins.
- Pass out a card to each child.
- Children give their cards to the banker.
- For 64¢, the banker gives out 6 dimes and 4 pennies.

Workbook Page: The children finish the page independently.

LESON 16. Test

Purpose: To test knowledge of the composition of 2-place numbers and ability to determine the total value of several coins.

Group Activity
I'm Thinking of a Number
Materials: Give the following to each of four children: A) dual board, five 10-blocks, and some cubes; B) number track, five 10-blocks, and number blocks 1 to 9; C) blocks with coins or just coins; and D) number markers 1 to 9 and 0

- Explain that a leader will think of a secret number and will announce the numbers it comes between, perhaps 1 and 30 (no number above 59).
- Have four children display their guesses with their materials.
- Have the rest of the children write their guesses on paper.
- The child whose guess is the closest to the secret number is the next leader.

Workbook Page: **A.** Go over the picture and first example.
B. Check that children understand the task.
C. Review the composition of teen numbers, showing they are built from 1 ten and some ones.
The children complete the test independently.

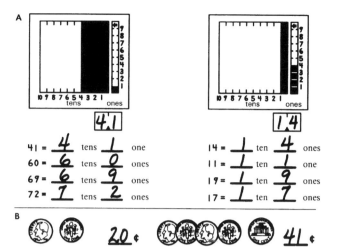

A

41 = _4_ tens _1_ one
60 = _6_ tens _0_ ones
69 = _6_ tens _9_ ones
72 = _7_ tens _2_ ones

14 = _1_ ten _4_ ones
11 = _1_ ten _1_ one
19 = _1_ ten _9_ ones
17 = _1_ ten _7_ ones

B

_20_ ¢   _41_ ¢
_12_ ¢   _14_ ¢

C

10 + 2 = _12_
10 + 8 = _18_
10 + 6 = _16_
10 + _3_ = 13
10 + _10_ = 20
10 + _4_ = 14

12 − 2 = _10_
19 − 9 = _10_
11 − 1 = _10_
18 − _8_ = 10
14 − _4_ = 10
17 − _7_ = 10

UNIT 4. PROBLEM SOLVING

Lessons in this unit:
17. Finding the Sum
18. Finding How Many Are Left
19. Finding How Many More Are Needed
20. Finding the Rest
21. Finding the Difference
22. Test

Arithmetic problems in first and second grade are solved by addition or subtraction. To help children solve these problems, teachers often provide verbal clues such as, to find how many more, subtract. However, children soon discover that such clues are not reliable.

Most children seem to recognize which problems can be solved by addition; it is usually the ones to be solved by subtraction that they cannot understand.

Children must be able to perceive each situation clearly so that they can interpret what is going on. They must understand the relationships and not be distracted by the numbers, which differ from problem to problem. By using materials to structure the situation described, they learn to read the text of the problem and to extract an equation with which to solve it.

The organization of problems into three basic types (described below) helps children understand why and when they solve a problem by addition or by subtraction.

Building a Foundation in Problem Solving

Problem solving in arithmetic involves applying knowledge of numbers and number relationships to questions that arise in daily life or to questions printed in workbook problems. Even before they are in school, children are aware that numbers play an important role in their lives. Once in school, they see numbers embedded in the text of the workbooks. For many children it is difficult to know how they can use the number facts they have learned in order to solve word problems. The examples are not already set up with numbers and signs. In fact, the operation to be used is never stated. From the very beginning, teachers should be aware of how difficult solving word problems appears to children. They can help children think through problems by acting them out with materials. Once children have learned to reason by structuring a situation in their minds, they can write the equation. We call this extracting an equation from the text. They then solve it to find the answer to the given question.

It is important for children to invent their own problems with the help of materials. In their imaginations, the blocks and cubes stand for animals or toys or any objects their minds create. The children's own problems switch easily from addition to subtraction. By acting out the problems, they show that they understand which operation is being used. Watching this process gives the teacher new insights into the level of understanding of their pupils.

One day the children no longer need the blocks. They are able to see the number relationships and solve the problems in their minds or by writing examples on paper.

Analysis of Problem Solving in Addition and Subtraction

There are three basic types of word problems: Type 1 requires addition, and types 2 and 3, subtraction, for their solution.

Type 1. Finding the Sum (taught in Lesson 17)

Two or more addends are given; the sum is found by addition. The result will be more. Example: Rob has 3 marbles. He wins 7 more. How many marbles does he have then? ($3 + 7 = 10$). The answer in context is Rob has 10 marbles.

Type 2. Finding How Many Are Left (taught in Lesson 18)

An amount is given which is then decreased by a certain amount; the remainder is found by subtraction. The result will be less. Example: Rob had 10 marbles. He lost 7 of them. How many marbles does he still have? The answer in context is Rob has 3 marbles left.

Types 3A, 3B, and 3C.

Type 3 problems are similar to each other in that a total and one part are given and the other part is to be found. The other part is found by subtracting the given part from the total.

Type 3 problems often confuse children because the situations do not seem to call for subtraction. To most children subtraction means that something is taken away or lost, yet the wording of type 3 problems never suggests anything has been diminished or lost. Before children can solve these problems, they must understand when to use subtraction—when a total and one part are given and the other part is to be found. The first step, then, is to help children identify type 3 problems.

Type 3A. Finding How Many More Are Needed (Lesson 19)

Type 3A problems state a total (such as a number of dollars unearned or pots unfilled) and one part (the part that is on hand or finished); the question is How many more are needed? For children, it seems to go against common sense to "take away" the amount that is on hand or finished! When problems are taught with small numbers, children easily solve them in their heads. They say, "I know the answer, but I don't know how I got it!" Here is an example: "The cook has 5 eggs. How many more does she need if the recipe calls for 9 eggs?" Children think $5 + \_\_ = 9$ and know the answer because they have learned that combination.

Most problems, however, use numbers so large that children cannot give the answer immediately. An example of this is "Juanita has $25 in her wallet. How much more money does she need to buy a TV set for $117?" If children write $25 + \_\_ = 117$, they can't automatically give the answer, for they don't know the combination. But if they realize that this is a type 3 problem, they can subtract the given part from the total to find the amount needed, writing it in column form.

$$\begin{array}{r} \$117 \\ -25 \\ \hline \$92 \end{array}$$

Type 3B. Finding the Rest

Type 3B problems also give the total and one part; the other part has to be found. The problem does not indicate that anything has been lost, so children may not think of subtracting. For example, "Rob has 16 marbles. 10 are blue; the rest are red. How many marbles are red?" This problem can be demonstrated by 16 cubes used to represent the marbles. The teacher says, "There are 10 blue marbles; we know this part" and covers up 10 cubes. "If we subtract the part we know from the total, we can find the rest" ($16 - 10 = 6$; 6 marbles are red).

Type 3C. Finding the Difference

In type 3C problems two amounts are compared—those that belong to A and those that belong to B. The question is either How much more does A have? or How much less does B have? Students learn that they are finding the difference. For example, "A has 9 marbles; B has 20. How many more marbles does B have?" The teacher places the totals of each (represented by blocks) side by side, and covers up the amount they have in common (9). The difference is thus found by subtracting the smaller amount from the larger ($20 - 9 = 11$; B has 11 more marbles than A).

All type 3 problems should be demonstrated in such a way that children understand that they should be solved by subtraction. They can easily identify the total—it's the largest number. They must remember that to find the unknown part, they subtract the given part from the total. Successful ways to teach type 3 problems are illustrated in the Games and Demonstrations section.

GAMES AND DEMONSTRATIONS

Finding How Many Are Left (use with Lesson 18)
Note: Type 2 problems tell about an amount that is decreased by being cut off or lost. The question is How much is left? or How much remains? (called the remainder).
Materials: number track 1 to 20, number blocks 1 to 10, cubes

* State the problem: "The shop had 12 tulips" (put blocks for 12 in the track).
* Continue, "It sold 2 tulips. How many tulips were left?"
* Ask a child, "Could you show us that example?"
* The child removes the 2-block and says, "12 minus 2 leaves 10. 10 tulips are left."
* In this situation the child finds it sensible to subtract since something was taken away or sold.
* A child writes the equation: 12 − 2 = 10.
* Another child answers in context, "The shop had 10 tulips left."

Note: The aim of the demonstration is to teach children to think through the actions involved. To keep them from depending on the verbal clue "How many are left?" ask the question in different ways—"How many did they keep?" or "How many did the store have then?"

Finding How Many More Are Needed (use with Lesson 19)
Note: In the wording of this type 3A problem, no amount becomes less. Instead, the question asks, "How many more are needed?" Carry out demonstrations with different materials. Your aim is to have the children see that the total consists of two parts and that it makes sense to subtract the given part from the total to find the other part.
Materials: number track 1 to 20, number blocks, cubes

* State the problem, "Neema has 16 flower pots to fill." (Put 16 cubes in the track. This is the total.)
* Say, "She put bulbs in 10 pots. That part is finished. Cover it up!" (do so).
* Ask, "How many more bulbs does she need for the rest?" (Point to the unfilled pots; this is the other part.)
* Call on a child to state the equation, "16 minus 10 leaves 6; Neema needs 6 more bulbs."
* Elicit that the child subtracted the covered part (which was given) from the total to find the other part (the unfilled pots).
* Let children invent problems in which someone must find how many more are needed, demonstrate them in the number track, and solve them on the chalkboard.

GAMES AND DEMONSTRATIONS

Finding the Rest (use with Lesson 20)

Note: The aim of the demonstration is to show that in a type 3B problem like this it makes sense to subtract the known part from the total to find the unknown part. To indicate subtraction, cover up the known part with a scarf. This allows the children to recognize that "the rest" is the unknown part.

Materials: number track 1 to 20, number blocks 1 to 10, cubes

* State the problem, "There are 16 children on the school bus." (Put 16 cubes in the track. This is the total.)
* Continue, "10 are girls; the rest are boys. How many boys are there?"
* Explain, "If I hide the number of girls, the rest are boys." (Cover the number of girls; point to the other part, the rest.)
* Ask, "Who can write this example?"
* A child writes the equation, 16 − 10 = 6, reads it, and puts the answer in context, "There are 6 boys."

Finding the Difference (use with Lesson 21)

Note: In type 3C problems, to find the difference between two amounts, you subtract the amount the two have in common from the larger amount.

Materials: two sets of number blocks

* State the problem, "Jack won 10 pennies" (put the 10-block on the table).
* Continue, "Jill won 14 pennies" (place the blocks for 10 and 4 next to the 10-block).
* Ask, "How many more pennies did Jill win?"
* Say, "I cover up the part that is the same" (do so by covering both 10-blocks).
* Say, "Now we see how much more Jill won."
* Explain that we call this "the difference."
* Call on a child to explain how to solve this problem.
* The child says, "14 minus 10 leaves 4. Jill won 4 more pennies."

ORAL PRACTICE IN SOLVING WORD PROBLEMS

You can change the numbers in the problems below. It is the structure that is important. Use these problems to give additional practice in problem solving. Have the children demonstrate them if possible.

Type 3A. To find how many more are needed, subtract the given part from the total (see Lesson 19)

1. Glen wants to own a dozen toy cars. She has 9 cars already. How many more cars does she need?
2. There are 20 steps in the ladder to the attic. Rafael is on the 12th step. How many more steps does he have to climb?
3. The twins said they would make 20 birthday cards. They finished 10 cards by lunch time. How many more cards do they still have to make?
4. A loaf of bread takes 20 minutes to bake. The bread has been baking for 12 minutes. How many more minutes must it bake?
5. Joy needs $18 to buy a toy boat. She has $3 in her bank. How much more money does she need to buy the boat?

Type 3B. To find the rest, subtract the part given from the total (see Lesson 20)

1. The pet shop had 19 cages. 6 cages had birds in them. The rest were empty. How many empty cages were there?
2. There were 14 candles on Shivonne's birthday cake. She blew out 10 candles. The rest were still burning. How many candles were still burning?
3. There were 16 children at the beach party. 10 children played tag. The rest went on a hike. How many children went on the hike?
4. There are 14 books on the shelf. The librarian gave the kids 4 books to read. They will get the rest tomorrow. How many books will they get tomorrow?

Type 3B. To find the rest of the distance, subtract the part traveled from the total number of miles in the trip

1. It is 18 miles from Jen's house to the beach. She drove 12 miles and stopped for lunch. How many miles was the rest of the trip?
2. Ms. Mendez drives 19 miles to work. After 2 miles she picks up her friend. She drives the rest of the way with her friend. How many miles is that?
3. Mr. DeMarco lives 13 miles from town. Jack gave him a lift for 10 miles. How far did he have to walk?

Type 3C. To find the difference between two amounts, subtract the amount they have in common from the larger number (see Lesson 21)

1. Kate took 14 books from the library. Darrell took out 16 books. How many more books did Darrell take out?
2. Mika made 15 paintings. Keisha made 10. How many more paintings did Mika make?
3. At the party 10 children wanted apple juice and 8 children wanted orange juice. How many more cups of apple juice did the children want?
4. There were 12 rainy days last month and 18 sunny days. How many more sunny days were there?

LESSON 17. Finding the Sum

Purpose: To solve problems of finding the sum and to recognize that these problems are solved by addition.
Group Activity
Using the Pattern Boards and Cubes (Set A)
Materials: pattern boards 1 to 10, cubes (build the cube patterns on pieces of paper if you do not have pattern boards)
- Say, "Mary had 10 cars" (build the 10-pattern).
- "She got 4 more cars" (build the 4-pattern and add it to the end of the 10-pattern).
- Ask, "How many cars did Mary have then?"
- Elicit that we add because there is more in the end.
- A child writes the example in column form and answers in context, "Mary had 14 cars then."

Using Blocks in the Number Track
Materials: number track, number blocks 1 to 10
- Children take turns inventing a story and demonstrating it by adding blocks in the number track.

Workbook Page: Read the examples for children who cannot read yet. Guide them in writing the numbers in the boxes provided and putting the answers in the sentence below the boxes.

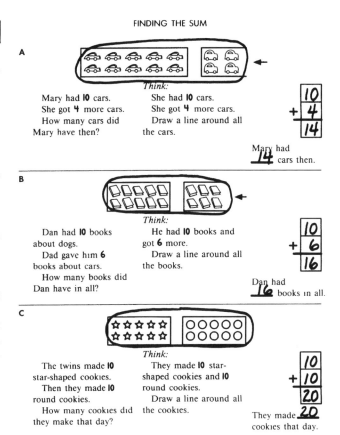

LESSON 18. Finding How Many Are Left

Purpose: To solve problems of finding how many are left (remainder) and to recognize that they are solved by subtraction.
Note: Encourage children to invent problems. First the storyteller must decide on a total (a teen number) and then separate it into two parts, one to be subtracted, the other to remain. The child demonstrates it with the materials and records it with numbers in column form.

Group Activity
Using the Pattern Boards and Cubes (Set A)
Materials: pattern boards 1 to 10 (or paper strips), cubes
- Say, "The shop had 12 tulips. It sold 2 tulips. How many tulips were left?"
- Build the 10-pattern and 2-pattern with cubes.
- A child subtracts 2 cubes and writes:

$$\begin{array}{r} 12 \\ -2 \\ \hline 10 \end{array}$$

- He states, "10 tulips were left."

Finding How Many Are Left—Using the Number Track
(see p. 26)
Materials: number track, number blocks 1 to 10
- Children invent subtraction stories in which something is sold or lost and demonstrate them with blocks.

Workbook Page: A. Go over the example; children cross out 2 tulips.
B and **C.** The children finish the page independently.

FINDING HOW MANY ARE LEFT

A
The shop had **12** tulips.
It sold **2** tulips.
How many tulips were left?

Think:
The shop had **12** tulips.
Cross out the tulips it sold.
The rest were left.

$$\begin{array}{r} 12 \\ -2 \\ \hline 10 \end{array}$$

The shop had _10_ tulips left.

B
Jed had **18¢**.
On the way to school he lost **8¢**.
How much money did he have left?

Think:
He had **18¢**.
Cross out the money he lost.

$$\begin{array}{r} 18 \\ -8 \\ \hline 10 \end{array}$$

Jed still had _10_ ¢.

C
The pet shop had **13** birds.
It sold **3** birds.
How many birds were left?

Think:
There were **13** birds.
Cross out the birds sold.
The rest were left in the shop.

$$\begin{array}{r} 13 \\ -3 \\ \hline 10 \end{array}$$

There were _10_ birds left.

LESSON 19. Finding How Many More Are Needed

Purpose: To solve problems of finding how many more are needed and to recognize that they are solved by subtraction.
Note: Children often have difficulty with these problems.

Group Activity
Using Pattern Boards and Cubes (Set A)
Materials: pattern boards 1 to 10 (or paper strips), cubes
- Say, "Neema has 16 flower pots to fill" (build the 10-pattern and the 6-pattern with cubes).
- Continue, "She put bulbs in 10 of the pots. These pots have been filled!" (cover the 10-pattern).
- Ask, "How many more bulbs does she need for the rest of the pots?" (point to the 6-pattern).
- Elicit that we subtract to find the other part; call on a child to write the example on the chalkboard.

$$\begin{array}{r} 16 \\ -10 \\ \hline 6 \end{array}$$

- The child states, "Neema needs 6 more bulbs."

Finding How Many More Are Needed—Using the Number Track (see p. 26)

Workbook Page: A. Go over the example carefully with the children.
B and **C.** The children finish the page independently.

FINDING HOW MANY MORE ARE NEEDED

A
Neema has **16** flower pots to fill.
She put bulbs in **10** of the pots.
How many more bulbs does she need for the rest of the pots?

Think:
She had **16** pots.
She filled **10** pots.
Cross out the pots she filled.

$$\begin{array}{r} 16 \\ -10 \\ \hline 6 \end{array}$$

Neema needs _6_ more bulbs.

B
Maria needs **$14** to buy a toy boat.
She has **$10** in her bank.
How much more money does she need?

Think:
The boat costs **$14**
Maria has **$10**
Cross out the part she already has.

$$\begin{array}{r} 14 \\ -10 \\ \hline 4 \end{array}$$

Maria needs $ _4_ more.

C
13 children are coming to Ben's party.
He has **10** chairs.
How many more chairs does he need?

Think:
Ben needs **13** chairs for the party.
He has **10** chairs.
Cross out the chairs he already has.

$$\begin{array}{r} 13 \\ -10 \\ \hline 3 \end{array}$$

Ben needs _3_ more chairs.

LESSON 20. Finding the Rest

Purpose: To solve problems of finding the rest and to recognize that they are solved by subtraction.
Group Activity
Using the Pattern Boards and Cubes (Set A)
Materials: pattern boards 1 to 20 (or paper strips), cubes
- Say, "Sandy picked 13 apples" (build the 10-pattern and the 3-pattern with cubes).
- Say, "10 apples were green; how many were red?"
- Cover, or move away, the part we know: the 10 apples.
- Elicit that we subtract one part to find the other part.
- Call on a child to write the example.

$$\begin{array}{r} 13 \\ -10 \\ \hline 3 \end{array}$$

- A child answers in context, "Sandy picked 3 red apples."

Finding the Rest (see p. 27)
- Help children tell stories in which there are two parts with different characteristics (see p. 28).
- Children demonstrate them with the blocks and solve them by subtracting the known part from the total.

Workbook Page: **A.** Go over the example and how to record it.
B. The children do this problem independently.

FINDING THE REST

A

Sandy picked 16 apples.
10 apples were green.
The others were red.
How many apples were red?

Think:
There were 16 apples.
Cross out the green apples.
The others were red.

$$\begin{array}{r} 16 \\ -10 \\ \hline 6 \end{array}$$

Sandy picked __6__ red apples.

B

Chris has 12 kittens.
2 kittens are gray.
The rest are white.
How many kittens are white?

Think
Chris has 12 kittens.
Cross out the gray kittens.
The rest are white.

$$\begin{array}{r} 12 \\ -2 \\ \hline 10 \end{array}$$

Chris has __10__ white kittens.

LESSON 21. Finding the Difference

Purpose: To find the difference between two amounts by subtracting what they have in common, that is, by subtracting the smaller from the larger number.
Group Activity
Finding the Difference—Using Blocks (see p. 27)
Using Cubes
Materials: cubes
- Say, "The bigger store has 13 floors" (make a row of 13 cubes).
- Say, "The smaller store has 10 floors" (make a row of 10 cubes alongside the 13 cubes).
- Ask, "How many more floors does the bigger store have?"
- Remind the children that up to 10 floors they are the same (cover the 10 cubes, the amount they have in common).
- Elicit that they can see the difference.
- The children subtract the smaller number from the bigger number to find the difference.
- In context, "The bigger store has 3 more floors."

What Is the Difference?
Materials: number blocks 1 to 10, ten 10-blocks, index cards with numbers 1 to 20
- Turn cards facedown.
- A child draws two cards, invents a story of finding the difference, and demonstrates it with the blocks.

Workbook Page: **A.** Go over the problem carefully.
B. The children finish the page independently.

FINDING THE DIFFERENCE

A

The bigger store has 13 floors.
The smaller store has 10 floors.
How many more floors does the bigger store have?

Think:
The bigger store has 13 floors.
Subtract the number of floors that is the same.

$$\begin{array}{r} 13 \\ -10 \\ \hline 3 \end{array}$$

The bigger store has __3__ more floors.

B

The big ladder has 15 steps.
The slide has 10 steps.
How many more steps does the ladder have?

Think.
The ladder has 15 steps.
Subtract the number of steps that is the same.

$$\begin{array}{r} 15 \\ -10 \\ \hline 5 \end{array}$$

The ladder has __5__ more steps.

LESSON 22. Test

Purpose: To test ability to solve word problems that require either addition or subtraction for their solution.

Group Activity

Materials: index cards with problems printed on them (see p. 28)
- Divide the class into two teams and turn the cards facedown.
- A player draws a card, reads the problem, writes the example on the chalkboard, and labels the answer.
- The answer becomes that player's score for his team.
- Ask players to demonstrate their problems with the materials if they still need the practice.

Workbook Page: If the children's ability to read is poor, write the difficult words on the board and go over them before they take the test: marbles, more, first, Rollo, money, party, favors, Paul, houses, bird, found. Remind children that they have to write the plus or minus sign in each example.
The children finish the page independently.

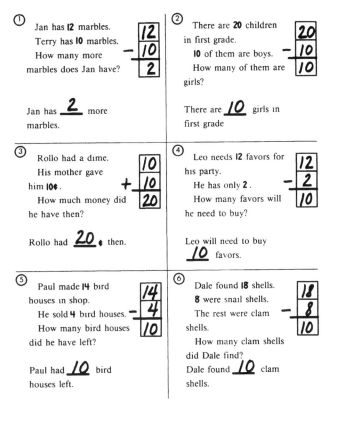

UNIT 5. TWO-PLACE NUMBERS IN THE NUMBER TRACK

Lessons in this unit:
23. Studying Numbers 1 to 100
24. How Far Will It Reach?
25. Breaking Two-Place Numbers into Tens and Ones
26. Less Than; Greater Than
27. Calendar

The Structure of Two-Place Numbers

In Unit 2 children began their study of 2-place numbers by building them in the dual board with tens and ones. Thus, they began by first understanding the structure of 2-place numbers and from that structure learning the place value system of notation. They built a number such as 29 with blocks and then recorded the number by placing the numeral 2 in the tens place. They found that even though 2 is a small number it stands for a larger size when it is in the tens position, and even though 9 seems large, it stands for a small size. Children learned visually that the value of each numeral is determined by its place in a 2-place number.

Two-Place Numbers in the Number Track

In Unit 5 children will put together the number track and discover that the series of numbers from 1 to 100 is divided into 10 sections, which are called *decades*. The word *decade* has the same root as *decimal*—the Latin word *decem*. This comes from our number system's being based on 10. Since the children already know where each number comes in the series from 1 to 10, they transfer this knowledge to the decades. They reason that if 4 comes after 3, then the 40s must come after the 30s. They figure that the last decade must be the 90s, the 20s come near the beginning, and the 50s must be in the middle.

Ordinal and Cardinal Aspects of the Numbers

Most children know how to count to one hundred, but are unaware of any meaning behind the number names. Once they count the units in the number track, they understand the concept behind the rhythm of the names. They realize that they are going from one to nine in each decade before they go on to the next decade. They are learning how to find the place of each number in the series from 1 to 100. This is the *ordinal* aspect of the number.

The children then take a number from the dual board where they can see how it is built and transfer it to the number track. Thus they "stretch out" a number such as 48, and find that each 10-block fills a decade of the track, bringing the number into the decade of the 40s where the 8-block reaches to 48.

Pointing to 48 in the track shows only one aspect, its *place* in the series—after 45, closer to 50 (ordinal aspect). When the blocks are put into the track, they show the *size* of 48 (cardinal aspect).

Rounding Off Numbers

The structure of the number track helps children understand the reasoning behind the rule for rounding off: when the ones digit in a 2-place number is 5 or bigger, you can round it off to the next higher ten. This rule may make little sense to children until they understand the structure of 2-place numbers. By placing the blocks for a number such as 48 in the number track, children can see how close 48 is to 50 and that 5 tens would be a convenient way to think of 4 tens, 8 ones. The same can be shown with 51. It is easier to think of it as 50.

GAMES AND DEMONSTRATIONS

How Far Will This Number Reach? (use with Lesson 24)
Note: In these lessons the children are learning the difference between the cardinal and the ordinal aspects of numbers. However, they need not learn the terms.
Materials: dual board, number track, 10-blocks, number blocks 1 to 9, number markers

- In the dual board build the 2-place number 28.
- Say, "These blocks show the size of 28."
* Label the blocks with the number markers for 28.
- Call on a child. Ask, "How far will this number reach in the track?" (The child points to 28 and says, "To 28.")
- Explain that this is the place of number 28 in the number sequence.
- Ask a child to place the blocks for 28 in the track and check that they do reach 28.
- Next, reverse the number markers 28 to form 82.
- Call on a child to build 82 in the dual board, name it, and locate its place in the number track.
- Give children the role of teacher. A child chooses two number markers and calls on a friend to first build a 2-place number with blocks, and then to reverse the numerals and build the new number.

LESSON 23. Studying Numbers 1 to 100

Purpose: To discover the place of each number in the number sequence from 1 to 100.
Group Activity
Materials: number track

- Separate the sections of the track and pass them out.
- To put the track together again ask, "Who has the first section? The teen numbers? The twenties? What comes after the 20s?" and so forth.
- Ask children to locate quickly numbers such as 39, 42, 25, 16, and 99 by pointing to each number on the track.

Workbook Page:

- Direct children to run a finger along each section of the track going from left to right.
- Ask children to write in the following numbers to check that they understand the meaning of *after*, *before*, and *between*:
  The number that comes after 5, after 15, after 25, after 35.
  The number that comes before 5, before 15, before 25, before 35.
  The number that comes between 2 and 4, between 12 and 14, between 22 and 24, between 32 and 34.
- The children write the rest of the numbers in sequence independently.

STUDYING NUMBERS 1 TO 100

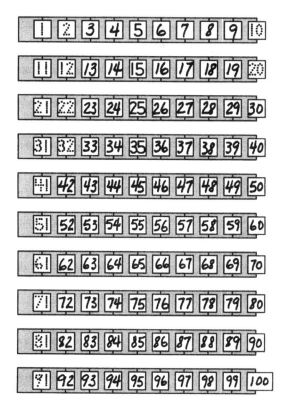

LESSON 24. How Far Will It Reach?

Purpose: To study the ordinal and cardinal aspects of numbers.

Note: When children construct with tens and ones two numbers that are reversals of one another (82 and 28), it sharpens their awareness of the amounts the numbers stand for. When they find the numbers' places in the number track, they confirm this. These experiences help prevent their making reversals.

Group Activity
How Far Will This Number Reach? (see p. 33)
Larger Number, Smaller Number
Materials: dual board, 10-blocks, number blocks 1 to 9, two sets number markers 1 to 9 and 0

- Turn number markers facedown.
- On the chalkboard, write two headings:
  Larger Number   Smaller Number
- A child selects two number markers, perhaps 9 and 1.
- She goes to the chalkboard and writes 91 under Larger Number and then 19 under Smaller Number.
- Another child builds each of these numbers in the dual board with the blocks and locates them in the track.

Workbook Page: Go over the first example. The children finish the page independently.

HOW FAR WILL IT REACH?

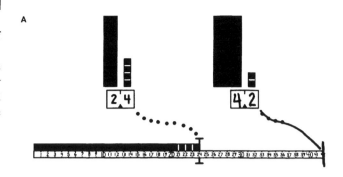

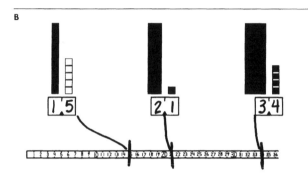

LESSON 25. Breaking Two-Place Numbers into Tens and Ones

Purpose: To record the addition and subtraction facts that result when 2-place numbers are broken into tens and ones.

Group Activity
Materials: dual board, number track, number markers, ten 10-blocks, number blocks 1 to 9

- Form the number 38 with two number markers.
- On the chalkboard write two headings, each with an example:

  Addition Fact   Subtraction Fact
  30 + 8 = 38   38 − 8 = 30

- The children take turns choosing a 2-place number and then building it in the dual board or in the number track.
- Ask each child to demonstrate one addition equation and one subtraction equation using that number and to write each equation under the correct heading.

Workbook Page: A and B. Elicit that each picture illustrates one of the facts written below it.
The children finish the page independently.

BREAKING TWO-PLACE NUMBERS INTO TENS AND ONES

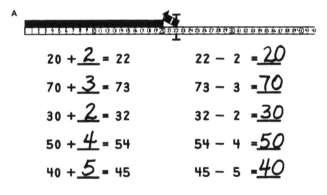

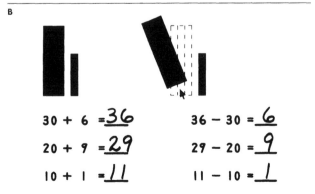

LESSON 26. Less Than; Greater Than

Purpose: To teach the meaning of the signs for *less than* and *greater than* and to compare them with the equal sign.

Group Activity
- On the chalkboard, draw a 2-block next to a 2-block.
- With colored chalk draw parallel lines like an equal sign—one bar connects the tops of the blocks, the other connects the bottoms of the blocks as in the workbook.
- Say, "This is an equal sign. We write 2 = 2."
- Draw a 2-block, and to the right of it, a 3-block.
- Draw lines that go from the small to the larger block, one line slanting up, the other slanting down.
- Write 2 < 3 and say, "We read this '2 is less than 3.'"
- Ask children to trace this sign with a finger between two blocks of different sizes.
- Reverse the position of the blocks in your drawing.
- Write 3 > 2 and read this as, "3 is greater than 2."
- Explain that a child once suggested the following as a good way to remember which way the sign goes, "The big number points to the little number."

Workbook Page: **A** and **B**. Go over the directions carefully.
B and **C**. The children finish the page independently.

LESS THAN; GREATER THAN

A

2 = 2	2 < 3	3 > 2
2 equals 2	2 is less than 3	3 is greater than 2

B Less than   2 ◯ 6   Greater than   6 ◯ 3

Think:
 2 is smaller than 6.
 Put one dot next to 2 ◯ 6
 the **2**.
 Put two dots next to 2 ⦂ 6
 the **6**.
 Connect the dots.   2 < 6

Think:
 6 is greater than 3.
 Put two dots next to 6 ⦂ 3
 the **6**.
 Put one dot next to 6 ◯ 3
 the **3**.
 Connect the dots.   6 > 3

5 < 10   6 > 2
6 < 8   8 > 5
3 < 5   5 > 3

C Write = or > or <.

5 = 5   6 < 10   8 > 3   34 = 34
3 < 7   2 < 8   4 < 6   26 < 29
7 > 2   9 > 5   9 = 9   11 > 10

LESSON 27. Calendar

Purpose: To study the structure of the calendar.

Group Activity
- Draw a blank calendar on the chalkboard.
- Write in the names of the days of the week.
- Elicit that each row of the calendar begins on Sunday.
- Have someone name the first school day of the week.
- Elicit the names of the days of the weekend.
- Teach the names of the days in the week; hide one name to see if they can remember it.
- Tell the children, "We are going to make this into the calendar for this month."
- Have a child write 1 in the correct square and fill in the squares till Saturday.
- Have another child fill in the next week, and so on.
- Once the numbers are in place, call on children to answer questions such as those for Lesson 27.
- Ask for birthdays and holidays during the month.

Workbook Page: The children write the name of the present month on the line at the top and fill in the numbers. Help with the questions if necessary.

CALENDAR

Sunday	Monday	Tuesday	Wednesday	Thursday	Friday	Saturday

Answers will vary.

① What is today's date?
Today is ──────── .

② What day of the week is the **7**th of this month?
The **7**th day is ────────

③ What is the date of the first Monday of this month?
────────

④ What is the date of the last day of this month?
────────

⑤ What are the dates of all the Sundays of this month?
────────

⑥ How many Mondays are there in this month?
──── Mondays

⑦ How many Thursdays are there in this month?
──── Thursdays

UNIT 6. SWITCHING FROM ONES TO TENS

Lessons in this unit:
28. Adding and Subtracting 1 Ten
29. Adding and Subtracting 2 Tens
30. Doubles
31. Finding One Half of a Double
32. Adding Neighbors
33. Subtracting Neighbors
34. Combinations That Make 100
35. Test

Adding and Subtracting Tens

In this unit children transfer the addition and subtraction facts from 1 to 10 to the next higher denomination—tens. They discover that facts such as 4 + 4 = 8 or 10 − 6 = 4 hold true with tens as well: 4 tens plus 4 tens make 8 tens, while 10 tens minus 6 tens leave 4 tens. As soon as children feel secure using the new number names, they have no difficulty solving simple oral problems such as "Forty and forty make what?" or "One hundred minus sixty leaves how much?" This is a result of having become thoroughly familiar with these concepts by handling the blocks before they turn to written work.

They realize they can add and subtract tens as easily as they could add and subtract ones. In this unit the basic groups of related facts studied in *Structural Arithmetic I* are reviewed in the new denomination. Thus, a basic combination such as 2 + 3 = 5 is reviewed as 20 + 30 = 50.

Mental Addition

It is important for children to be able to add simple 2-place numbers in their heads. It is the work with the materials that enables them to do so easily. It should never be necessary in doing daily tasks such as shopping to have to write simple additions down on paper. They should know that 50¢ plus 2 dimes is 70¢ or one dollar minus 20¢ is 80¢.

Mental Computation in Column Addition

When children learn to add in column form, an example such as 10 plus 30 is computed piecemeal. They say, "Zero and zero is zero; one and three is four." The answer comes out correctly, but the children may have no understanding that tens are involved. This makes it difficult for them to understand the concept of regrouping when they must learn how to "carry" or "borrow" one ten.

Mental computation is also used in adding long columns of numbers. A person must keep in mind the decade that is being added to. In the example 7 + 8 + 9 + 6 = ___ the mental work is as follows: (7 + 8) "fifteen," (+9) "twenty-four," (+6) "thirty." At each step one has to keep in mind the number of tens, or the decade one is working in.

Although calculators are prevalent, they are not instruments that lead to understanding numbers. In daily tasks such as reading the newspaper, too many people are totally in the dark when they read big numbers. For example, "$60 million was increased by 10% this year," has little real meaning for them. Today, children need more, not less, mental work with numbers to be able to fully understand the numbers they see printed everywhere.

Upper-Decade Facts

Throughout this book children will be asked to write facts they know transposed to higher decades. Drilling the same facts over and over again is deadening. However, a child who thinks up a similar fact in a higher decade not only masters the fact, but enjoys the feeling of being creative.

GAMES AND DEMONSTRATIONS

Stop-and-Go Game—Switching from Ones to Tens (use with lesson 28)

Note: Make a stop-and-go cube by coloring two sides of a cube red and four sides green. When this cube is tossed, the red side up means Stop and the green side means Go. In this game Go means the player may move his or her team's marker up 10 units in the number track.

Materials: number track 1 to 100, cubes for markers, stop-and-go cube

- Assign each team a cube of a special color as its marker.
- Each team places its marker on 0.
- The players take turns tossing the stop-and-go cube.
- In the illustration, team B's plays are not shown; team A has moved to 10, then to 20.
* Say, "You are on 20. Drop the stop-and-go cube. If you get Go, you can move your marker up 10."
- A child drops the cube and says, "Go! 20 and 10 is 30! I'm on 30 now!" (moves cube to 30).
- The winner is the first team to reach 100.

Note: Since red sometimes turns up too often, the following rule is a good idea: a player who throws Stop for the third time gets a free turn.

Hiding Game (use with Lesson 34)

Note: The children have mastered the combinations that make 10 by filling the 10-box with blocks. Check to see that they know these combinations.

Materials: dual board, ten 10-blocks

- Elicit that the dual board holds ten 10-blocks.
- Separate the 10-blocks so that the children can see that 9 tens and 1 ten make 10 tens, 8 tens plus 2 tens make 10 tens, and so on.
- Now ask the children to close their eyes.
- Hide behind you two groups of tens that together total 10 tens, perhaps 5 tens and 5 tens.
* Say, "Open your eyes. I have 10 tens altogether. In one hand I have 5 tens" (put them in the dual board).
- Ask, "What is in the other hand?"
- When a child answers, "5 tens!" display the 10-blocks you have hidden.
- Give these 5 tens to a child to put in the dual board.
- The child states, "5 tens and 5 tens make 10 tens."
- Encourage children to take the role of teacher in this game.

LESSON 28. Adding and Subtracting 1 Ten

Purpose: To discover that the concept of adding 1 and subtracting 1 can be transferred to tens, that is, adding 1 ten and subtracting 1 ten.

Group Activity
Materials: dual board, cubes, ten 10-blocks
- Review the +1 facts: $1 + 1 = 2, 2 + 1 = 3 \ldots 9 + 1 = 10$.
- Demonstrate the same facts with tens by adding 1 ten after another in the tens compartment.
- Have children recite each fact and write it: $10 + 10 = 20$, $20 + 10 = 30 \ldots 90 + 10 = 100$.
- Explain the writing of 10 tens; write $9 + 1 = 10$. Then write 0 after each number: $90 + 10 = 100$.
- Children demonstrate subtracting 1 ten from a number of tens and record equations on the chalkboard.

Stop-and-Go Game—Adding 10 (see p. 37)
- Play the Stop-and-Go Game with two teams.
- Then play by starting at 100 and subtracting 10 each time.

Workbook Page: A. Go over the picture of the demonstration.

B and **C.** Children think up similar equations in other decades.

ADDING AND SUBTRACTING 1 TEN

A
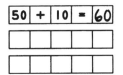

$3 + 1 = \underline{4}$ $30 + 10 = \underline{40}$

B Adding 10
Think up more +10 facts.
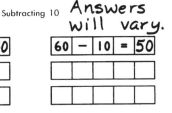

$40 + 10 = \underline{50}$ $50 + 10 = \underline{60}$

C Subtracting 10   Answers will vary.
Think up more −10 facts.

$50 - 10 = \underline{40}$ $60 - 10 = \underline{50}$

LESSON 29. Adding and Subtracting 2 Tens

Purpose: To discover that the concept of adding 2 and subtracting 2 can be transferred to tens, that is, adding 2 tens and subtracting 2 tens.

Group Activity
Materials: dual board, cubes, ten 10-blocks
- Review the +2 facts by adding 2 cubes to different numbers of cubes in the ones compartment.
- Switch to the tens compartment and show the same facts with tens: 2 tens + 2 tens = 4 tens, and so on.
- Children recite the facts, "Twenty and twenty make forty," and record them on the chalkboard: $20 + 20 = 40$.
- Call on children to demonstrate subtracting 2 tens from a number of tens and recording the equations.

Hiding Game—Adding or Subtracting 2 Tens
Materials: dual board, ten 10-blocks, scarf
- Place 8 ten-blocks in the dual board and cover them with a scarf.
- Say, "I have hidden 8 tens. If I subtract 2 tens (remove 2 tens), how many tens will be left?"
- Call on a child to answer and write the equation on the chalkboard: $80 - 20 = 60$. Remove the scarf to check.
- At the next turn, add 2 tens to the hidden tens and ask for the equation: $60 + 20 = 80$.

Workbook Page: The children finish the page independently.

ADDING AND SUBTRACTING 2 TENS

A
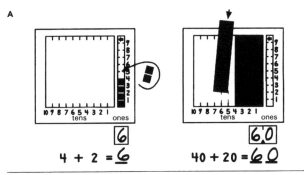

$4 + 2 = \underline{6}$ $40 + 20 = \underline{60}$

B Adding 20
Think up more +20 facts.
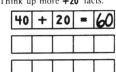 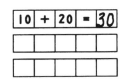

$40 + 20 = \underline{60}$ $10 + 20 = \underline{30}$

C Subtracting 20   Answers will vary.
Think up more −20 facts.
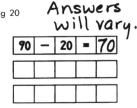

$80 - 20 = \underline{60}$ $90 - 20 = \underline{70}$

LESSON 30. Doubles

Purpose: To master the addition and subtraction facts dealing with the doubles of full tens.

Group Activity
Materials: dual board, cubes, 10-blocks
- Review the concept of doubles.
- Begin by placing 3 cubes in each hand.
- Ask, "If I have 3 cubes in each hand, how many do I have in all?"
- The child who answers, "6," writes the equation on the chalkboard: 3 + 3 = 6.
- Call on a child to show the same example with tens and write the equation on the chalkboard: 30 + 30 = 60.

Hiding Game—Subtracting from Doubles
Materials: 10-blocks
- While the children's eyes are closed, explain that you are hiding an equal number of tens in each hand.
- Say, "I have forty altogether. If I take one handful away, how much is left?"
- A child says, "40 minus 20 leaves 20" and writes the equation on the chalkboard.
- Encourage children to take the role of teacher.

Workbook Page: Go over the page. The children finish the page independently.

DOUBLES

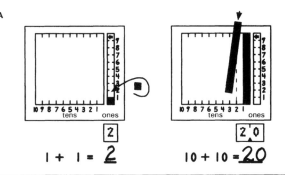

A

1 + 1 = 2   10 + 10 = 20

B   Addition

1 + 1 = 2   3 + 3 = 6
10 + 10 = 20   30 + 30 = 60

2 + 2 = 4   4 + 4 = 8
20 + 20 = 40   40 + 40 = 80

C   Subtraction

6 − 3 = 3   2 − 1 = 1
60 − 30 = 30   20 − 10 = 10

4 − 2 = 2   10 − 5 = 5
40 − 20 = 20   100 − 50 = 50

LESSON 31. Finding One Half of a Double

Purpose: To study the concept of one half and the meaning of the symbol $\frac{1}{2}$; to find one half of a double.

Group Activity
Materials: number blocks, ten 10-blocks
- Hold up a 3-block in each hand.
- Ask, "How much do I have altogether?" (6).
- Thrust one hand forward and explain, "One out of two equal parts is called one half."
- On the chalkboard write:

    1 out of
    2 equal parts

- Now erase the words, leaving the symbol for one half.
- Place 3 tens in each hand; elicit the total (6 tens).
- Say, "I give you one of the two equal parts" (do so).
- Ask, "Now what is one half of 60?" (30).
- Call on children to demonstrate one half of even amounts of tens and write the equations on the board:

    $\frac{1}{2}$ of 60 = ___ $\frac{1}{2}$ of 40 = ___ $\frac{1}{2}$ of 80 = ___

Workbook Page: **A, B,** and **C.** Go over the illustrations first. The children complete the examples.
D. Remind children how to solve for X (see Lesson 1).

FINDING ONE HALF OF A DOUBLE

A

We cut 4 into 2 parts.   We call 1 of the 2 parts one half.   We write: $\frac{1}{2}$ of 4 = 2

B

We cut 40 into 2 parts.   We call 1 of the 2 parts one half.   We write: $\frac{1}{2}$ of 40 = 20

C

$\frac{1}{2}$ of 60 is 30 . $\frac{1}{2}$ of 80 is 40 .
$\frac{1}{2}$ of 20 is 10 . $\frac{1}{2}$ of 40 is 20 .

D

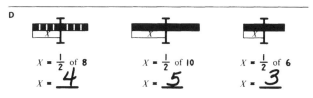

X = $\frac{1}{2}$ of 8   X = $\frac{1}{2}$ of 10   X = $\frac{1}{2}$ of 6
X = 4   X = 5   X = 3

LESSON 32. Adding Neighbors

Purpose: To discover that the combinations resulting from adding neighbors can be transferred to tens.

Group Activity

Cup Game

Materials: dual board, 10-blocks, cubes, two cups
- Review the addition facts called neighbors by playing the Cup Game. In one cup put 2 cubes, in the other, 3 cubes. As you dump them out, children say, "2 and 3 make 5."
- Demonstrate with tens: 2 tens and 3 tens make 5 tens.

Stop-and-Go Game

Materials: dual board, 10-blocks, stop-and-go cube
- Divide the children into teams A and B.
- When their eyes are closed, hide 2 tens and 3 tens.
- Say, "Open your eyes. I have 5 tens in all. The groups are neighbors."
- Ask team A, "How many tens are in each hand?"
- A player says, "2 tens and 3 tens" and places them in the dual board.
- She tosses the stop-and-go cube, gets Go, and writes an equation on the chalkboard for Team A.
- The first team with five equations wins.

Workbook Page: The children finish the page independently.

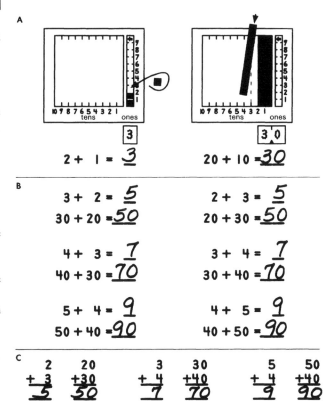

LESSON 33. Subtracting Neighbors

Purpose: To discover that the combinations resulting from subtracting one of a pair of neighbors from an odd number can be transferred to an odd number of tens.

Group Activity

Materials: dual board, ten 10-blocks, scarf
- On the chalkboard write two columns of examples.

Column A	Column B
30 − 10 = ___	30 − 20 = ___
50 − 20 = ___	50 − 30 = ___
70 − 30 = ___	70 − 40 = ___
90 − 40 = ___	90 − 50 = ___

- While the children's eyes are closed, place 5 tens in the dual board and hide them under a scarf.
- Say, "Open your eyes. I have hidden 5 tens; if I subtract 2 tens (do so), how many tens are left?"
- Call on a child to give the answer (3 tens) and lift up the scarf to verify it.
- The child goes to the board, locates the corresponding equation, and writes the answer: 50 − 20 = 30.
- Demonstrate each example on the chalkboard.

Workbook Page: The children finish the page independently.

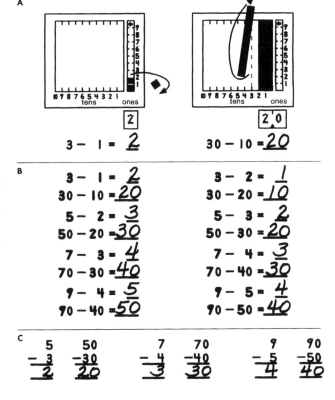

LESSON 34. Combinations That Make 100

Purpose: To discover that the knowledge of the addition and subtraction facts that make 10 can be transferred to the tens; the resulting combinations make 10 tens, or 100.

Group Activity

Materials: 10-box, number blocks, number track 1 to 10
- The children fill the 10-box to review the 10-facts.
- Display the first section of the number track.
- Demonstrate that the 9-block and 1-block make 10.
- Write 9 + 1 = 10 on the chalkboard.
- Now demonstrate the same combination with tens; stand them up vertically in the number track.
- Ask, "What do 9 tens need to make 10 tens?" (1 ten).
- Have a child go to the chalkboard and write both equations: 9 + 1 = 10 and below it, 90 + 10 = 100.
- With chalk, darken the numbers so the children can see **90 + 10 = 100**.
- Demonstrate other similar pairs of equations.

Hiding Game (see p. 37)
- This is a review of the 10-facts transferred to tens.

Workbook Page: Go over the illustration. The children finish the page independently.

A

9 + 1 = 10   90 + 10 = 100
1 + 9 = 10   10 + 90 = 100

B
8 + 2 = 10   6 + 4 = 10
80 + 20 = 100   60 + 40 = 100

7 + 3 = 10   5 + 5 = 10
70 + 30 = 100   50 + 50 = 100

C
50 + **50** = 100   60 + **40** = 100
30 + **70** = 100   20 + **80** = 100
40 + **60** = 100   70 + **30** = 100

LESSON 35. Test

Purpose: To test knowledge of the basic addition and subtraction facts when these facts have been transferred to full tens.

Group Activity

Note: Some children may still be weak in certain of the "difficult" facts. These are usually the facts resulting from adding or subtracting 2, or adding neighbors and the related subtraction facts. Use games on pages 8 to 10 to review basic facts.

Workbook Page: A. Let the children take turns picking out a difficult combination and then demonstrating it with tens. Have them write it on the chalkboard.

B. Go over the problems. If necessary, have the children solve similar problems you make up (see Finding the Sum, p. 28).

TEST

A
80 + 10 = **90**   90 − 20 = **70**   40 + 40 = **80**
30 + 30 = **60**   60 − 30 = **30**   70 − 10 = **60**
40 + 50 = **90**   100 − 30 = **70**   60 + 40 = **100**
70 + 30 = **100**   90 − 10 = **80**   20 + 30 = **50**

30 + 20 = **50**   50 − 20 = **30**   100 − 70 = **30**
60 + 20 = **80**   80 − 40 = **40**   80 − 20 = **60**
40 + 60 = **100**   40 − 10 = **30**   90 + 10 = **100**
50 + 50 = **100**   100 − 60 = **40**   80 − 40 = **40**

30 + 70 = **100**   40 − 40 = **0**   60 − 20 = **40**
70 + 20 = **90**   70 − 20 = **50**   40 + 30 = **70**
80 + 20 = **100**   100 − 40 = **60**   30 − 30 = **0**
50 + 20 = **70**   50 − 10 = **40**   30 + 40 = **70**

B
Tasha had **60¢**.
Her mother gave her **10¢** for putting out the trash.
How much money did Tasha have then?

Lina is **10** years old.
Ms. Green is **20** years older than Lina.
How old is Ms. Green?

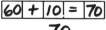   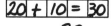

Tasha had **70**¢.   Ms. Green is **30** years old.

UNIT 7. ADDING AND SUBTRACTING TWO-PLACE NUMBERS

Lessons in this unit:
36. Finding the Total Distance
37. Finding the Rest of the Distance
38. Test
39. Adding 10 to Two-Place Numbers
40. Subtracting 10 from Two-Place Numbers
41. Adding and Subtracting Several Tens
42. Adding Two-Place Numbers
43. Subtracting Two-Place Numbers
44. Nickels and Dimes
45. Dimes and Dollars
46. Nickels, Dimes, and Dollars
47. Quarters and Half Dollars
48. Test

Solving Distance Problems

In the last unit children learned to add tens to tens (40 + 30 = 70). They will apply this knowledge to solving problems in distance, using both addition and subtraction examples.

Adding Full Tens to 2-Place Numbers

In Unit 7 children will learn to add full tens to any 2-place number (43 + 20). They will also learn to subtract full tens from any 2-place number (63 − 20).

Mental Computation

When children hear the example "forty-three plus forty," they naturally add the tens first; the ones remain the same. The answer is "eighty-three." To give pupils practice in mental computation the workbook puts the examples in equation form. Adding mentally is an important skill for column addition. The hidden steps in column addition are the mental adding of partial sums. In adding a long column of numbers, one must be able to keep the tens in mind. In adding the numbers in an example such as 9 + 8 + 7 + 9, one moves from the teens to the 20s to the 30s.

Written Computation

In Lesson 41 the children will learn that the approach used in written computation differs from that used in mental computation. As soon as column addition with 2-place numbers is introduced, they must learn how to figure written examples like this one:

$$\begin{array}{r} 43 \\ +40 \\ \hline \end{array}$$

From the very start they must learn to add the ones column first, thus saying "0 plus 3 is 3." Later, when regrouping is taught, they will understand why they start with the ones—because it enables them to "carry 1 ten" to the tens column when the sum of the ones column is greater than 10. The same procedure will be used in reverse in solving subtraction examples in written form.

Money

Lessons 44 to 47 teach the values of coins—nickels, dimes, quarters, and half-dollars—and the value of one dollar. Children study the relationships between the coins by pasting them on blocks which they then measure in the number track or dual board. The value of coins is always stated in cents. Since dimes are the tens of our monetary system, we know the value of a number of dimes immediately, 7 dimes = 70¢.

The children work with nickels pasted on 5-blocks. This shows that a nickel is worth half of 10¢. In the dual board, children group pairs of nickels together to form tens and can see for themselves that 5 nickels make 2 tens and 5 ones, or 25¢. Since a quarter is worth 25¢, they reason that a quarter equals 5 nickels.

The work with 5-blocks will be presented again in Unit 10. The children will learn to relate the time on the clock face to the digital method of recording time.

Money—A Foundation for Understanding Decimals

Children learn about the relationship between nickels, dimes, quarters, half-dollars, and 100¢ by measuring them in the number track 1 to 100. The experiments enable them to build a foundation that is basic to their understanding of decimal notation and percent, for example, a quarter = 25¢; in decimal notation, 25¢ = .25; put differently, $\frac{1}{4}$ = 25%.

By working with the blocks in the number track and in the dual board the children learn concepts through insight. These are concepts they can build on in more advanced arithmetic.

GAMES AND DEMONSTRATIONS

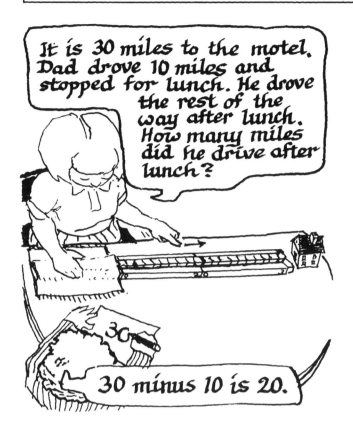

Finding the Rest of the Distance (use with Lesson 37)
Note: Some children find it difficult to understand that to find the rest of the distance, they must subtract the number of miles already driven from the total length of the trip. It is helpful if they can think of the total trip as being made up of two parts. Cover the first part with a scarf (the miles already driven). This lets them see the other part of the total; elicit that this part is the rest of the distance to be traveled. By covering one part you suggest subtracting it from the whole.

Materials: number track, 10-blocks, number blocks 1 to 9, scarf

* State the problem, "It is 30 miles to the motel" (put 3 tens in the track).
* Continue, "Dad drove 10 miles and stopped for lunch" (cover this part with a scarf).
* Say, "He drove the rest of the way after lunch. How many miles did he drive after lunch?" (point).
* Ask, "Who can tell us the equation?"
* A child says, "30 minus 10 is 20," writes it, and puts it in context, "Dad will drive 20 miles after lunch."

Coin Lotto (use for Lessons 45 to 47)
Materials: dual board, 10-blocks, 5-blocks, 8 cubes per child, 9 index cards, lotto cards

Cut out pictures of coins from workbooks and paste groups of coins on 9 index cards. The total value on each card is: 5¢, 10¢, 15¢, 20¢, 25¢, 30¢, 50¢, 60¢, and 75¢. Make two versions of lotto cards.

75¢	15¢	10¢	25¢
50¢	20¢	5¢	30¢

60¢	15¢	10¢	25¢
50¢	20¢	5¢	30¢

* Give a lotto card and 8 cubes to put on the 8 squares to each child.
* To win, a player must cover all 8 squares with cubes.
* Hold up the pictures of coins one after the other. Give children time to scan their lotto cards for the number of cents that records the total value of the coins in each picture.
* Select one pupil to construct the amount with blocks.
* Have the children check their totals with the blocks in the dual board. This structure helps them recall the values of the coins.

LESSON 36. Finding the Total Distance

Purpose: To solve problems of finding the total distance traveled and to recognize that these problems are solved by addition.

Group Activity
Materials: number track, 10-blocks
- Say, "Tama is driving to Big Pond."
- "She drives 20 miles and stops at a store."
- Have a child put 2 ten-blocks in the track.
- Continue, "Then she drives 30 more miles."
- Call on a child to add 3 tens to the 2 tens in the track.
- Ask, "How many miles does Tama drive?"
- Call on a child to explain what is happening in the problem.
- Elicit that we find the total distance by adding the two parts together: 20 + 30 = 50. Tama drives 50 miles.
- Have children make up problems of finding the total distance driven.

Workbook Page: A and B. The children finish the page independently.

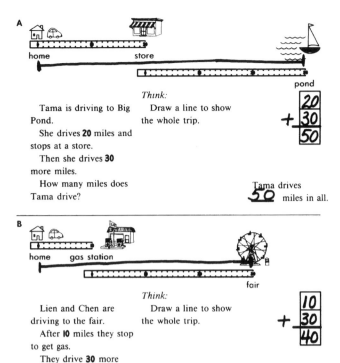

LESSON 37. Finding the Rest of the Distance

Purpose: To solve problems of finding the rest of the distance traveled and to recognize that these problems are solved by subtraction.

Group Activity
Finding the Rest of the Distance (see p. 43)
Card Game
Materials: number track, 10-blocks, number blocks 1 to 9, 8 index cards labeled 30, 40, 50 . . . 100
- Turn the cards facedown and let numbers be drawn.
- A player who chooses 60 must make up a problem in which 60 is the total distance of the trip.
- She decides how many miles are driven in the morning, asks the question "How many miles is the rest of the trip?" and demonstrates it in the number track.
- She writes the equation on the board, perhaps 60 − 30 = 30. The rest of the trip is 30 miles long.

Workbook Page: A and B. It is easy for the children to see that the part they cross off in the workbook is the part of the trip they subtract. They record the numbers in the space to the right and subtract to find the rest of the distance.

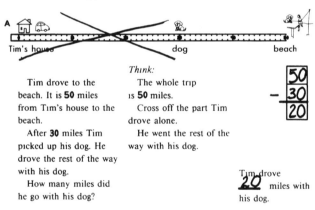

44

LESSON 38. Test

Purpose: To test ability to solve word problems that require either addition or subtraction for their solution.

Group Activity
Materials: index cards. Make a review game for problem solving by writing problems on cards. Use the problems on page 28, substituting larger numbers.
- Divide the class into two teams.
- A player draws a card, reads the problem, writes the example on the chalkboard, and labels the answer.
- The number in the answer is that player's score for his team.
- Some children may still need to demonstrate their problems with materials first.

Workbook Page
Have the children classify the problems ahead of time:
1. To find the rest of the distance (subtract)
2. To find the rest (subtract)
3. To find the whole trip (add)
4. To find the rest or the other part (subtract)
5. To find how many more (subtract)
6. To find the difference (subtract)

TEST

① It is **40** miles to Blue Lake.
 We went **10** miles by bus and the rest of the way by car.
 How many miles did we go by car?
 We went __30__ miles by car.

 40
− 10
 30

② There are **30** children on the playground.
 10 of them are girls.
 How many of them are boys?
 There are __20__ boys on the playground.

 30
− 10
 20

③ Joe rode his bike **20** miles to Jack's Snacks.
 He rode **10** more miles after his snack.
 How many miles did Joe ride in all?
 Joe rode __30__ miles.

 20
+ 10
 30

④ It is **40** miles from my house to the river.
 20 miles of the road were under water.
 How many miles were not under water?
 __20__ miles were not under water.

 40
− 20
 20

⑤ There were **80** steps to the top of the fire tower.
 We stopped to rest after **20** steps.
 How many more steps did we have to go?
 __60__ more steps

 80
− 20
 60

⑥ It is **50** miles from Gwen's house to the beach.
 It is **80** miles from Stan's house to the beach.
 How much closer does Gwen live to the beach than Stan?
 __30__ miles closer

 80
− 50
 30

LESSON 39. Adding 10 to Two-Place Numbers

Purpose: To discover that adding 10 to a 2-place number yields a number in the next higher decade with the same digit in the ones place.

Group Activity
Adding 10 in the Dual Board
Materials: dual board, cubes, 10-blocks
- In the dual board, build a number such as 46.
- Ask a child to add 10 to 46 (child adds 1 ten to the 4 tens).
- Elicit that the answer is 56 because there is 1 more ten, but the number of ones stays the same.
- Have children add 10 to other 2-place numbers.

Stop-and-Go Game Variation (see p. 37)
Materials: number track 1 to 100, cubes for markers, stop-and-go cube
- Choose teams and give each a colored cube.
- Each team puts its cube on a different number in the first decade of the number track.
- The players alternate tossing the stop-and-go cube and moving up 10 into the next decade.
- The winning team is the first to reach the 90s.

Workbook Page: Review solving for X (see Lesson 1). The children finish the page independently.

ADDING 10 TO TWO-PLACE NUMBERS

A
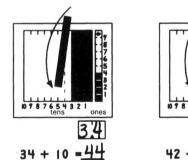 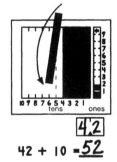

34
34 + 10 = __44__

42
42 + 10 = __52__

B You can do these in your head.

17 + 10 = __27__   61 + 10 = __71__
28 + 10 = __38__   89 + 10 = __99__
33 + 10 = __43__   76 + 10 = __86__
45 + 10 = __55__   57 + 10 = __67__

C Find X.

$X = 21 + 10$ $X = 13 + 10$ $X = 68 + 10$
$X = \underline{31}$ $X = \underline{23}$ $X = \underline{78}$

$X = 82 + 10$ $X = 39 + 10$ $X = 54 + 10$
$X = \underline{92}$ $X = \underline{49}$ $X = \underline{64}$

LESSON 40. Subtracting 10 from Two-Place Numbers

Purpose: To discover that subtracting 10 from a 2-place number yields a number in the next lower decade with the same digit in the ones place.

Group Activity
Stop-and-Go Game—Subtracting 10
Materials: dual board, twelve 10-blocks, two sets of number blocks 1 to 9, stop-and-go cube

- Divide the class into teams A and B.
- Give one team the dual board to build numbers in.
- The other team builds numbers in the chalk tray.
- Give each team 6 tens and blocks 1 to 9.
- Each team begins by building a large 2-digit number with these blocks (perhaps 68 and 65).
- Team A tosses the stop-and-go cube and gets Go.
- The player subtracts 1 ten from 6 tens and writes 68 − 10 = 58 under his team's name on the chalkboard.
- The winning team is the first to subtract all of its 10-blocks. The final equations will be 18 − 10 = 8 and 15 − 10 = 5.

Workbook Page: **A.** Go over the illustration.
B. Children work independently.
C. Make sure children know which equations to write.

SUBTRACTING 10 FROM TWO-PLACE NUMBERS

A
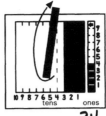

44 − 10 = _34_   34 − 10 = _24_

B You can do these in your head.

24 − 10 = _14_   69 − 10 = _59_
38 − 10 = _28_   35 − 10 = _25_
55 − 10 = _45_   48 − 10 = _38_
72 − 10 = _62_   93 − 10 = _83_

C Make up more −10 facts.

| 28 − 10 = 18 | | 16 − 10 = 6 | | 99 − 10 = 89 |

Answers will vary.

LESSON 41. Adding and Subtracting Several Tens

Purpose: To add or subtract several tens from a 2-place number in column form.

Group Activity
Note: At first it seems strange to children that they must add or subtract 2-place numbers by starting with the ones column on the right side. This goes against what they have been taught to do—start to read or write on the left side. However, they must practice starting with the ones column, as they will need to do this as soon as the sum exceeds 10 and regrouping becomes necessary.

Stop-and-Go Game
Materials: stop-and-go cube

- On the chalkboard, write two different sets of examples similar to those in the workbook. Label them Team A and Team B.
- Divide the class into teams A and B.
- The first player on Team A tosses the stop-and-go cube.
- If she gets Go, she adds the first example on the board, adding the ones first, then the tens.
- The first team to add all of its examples wins.

Workbook Page: The children finish the page independently.

ADDING AND SUBTRACTING SEVERAL TENS

A
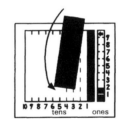

First add the ones.
Then add the tens.

```
tens ones
  1   2          1 2
+ 3   0        +3 0
  4   2          4 2
```

B
```
 38    21    47    56    72    65
+20   +40   +30   +40   +20   +20
 58    61    77    96    92    85
```

C First subtract the ones.
Then subtract the tens.

```
 49    51    83    28    65    77
-20   -30   -40   -20   -20   -60
 29    21    43     8    45    17
```

LESSON 42. Adding Two-Place Numbers

Purpose: To add two 2-place numbers written in column form.

Note: Remind children that when adding examples in column form, they must add ones to ones first, and then add tens to tens.

Group Activity

Materials: dual board, 10-blocks, cubes

- Select two children; give one child 5 ten-blocks and 5 cubes.
- Limit the other child to 4 ten-blocks and 4 cubes. (This assures that the total will be less than 10.)
- The first child builds a number with blocks and then writes it on the chalkboard (perhaps 45).
- The other child builds a number and writes it on the chalkboard below 45 (perhaps 43).
- A scribe adds the example:

$$\begin{array}{r} 45 \\ +43 \\ \hline 88 \end{array}$$

- The children check the answer (88) by adding the two sets of blocks in the dual board.
- Select other pairs of children to build numbers with blocks, add them together, and write the examples on the chalkboard.

Workbook Page: A. Go over the illustration.
B. The children finish the page independently.

LESSON 43. Subtracting Two-Place Numbers

Purpose: To subtract one 2-place number from another in column form.

Group Activity

Materials: dual board, 10-blocks, cubes

- Ask a child to build 76 in the dual board.
- Write a subtraction example on the board.

$$\begin{array}{r} 76 \\ -31 \end{array}$$

- The child subtracts the appropriate blocks from the 7 tens and 6 ones as you dictate, "6 minus 1 leaves . . . ?" (5 ones), "7 minus 3 leaves . . . ?" (4 tens). (45)
- To check: Place the number subtracted (3 tens, 1 cube) back in the dual board with 4 tens, 5 ones, to get 76. Show how to check the written example.

Subtraction Game

Materials: two boxes labeled Big Numbers and Small Numbers, number markers

- Put number markers 5 to 9 in the Big Numbers box and 0 to 4 in the Small Numbers box.
- Player A selects two markers from the Big Numbers box and forms a 2-place number (67), and then draws two markers from the Small Numbers box (43).
- A scribe writes the example in column form.
- The answer is the score; the biggest answers win.

Workbook Page: A and **B.** The children work independently.
C. Checking a subtraction example is explained above.

ADDING TWO-PLACE NUMBERS

A

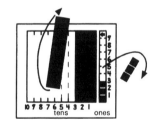

First add the ones.
Then add the tens.

tens ones
$$\begin{array}{r} 4\ 2 \\ +2\ 3 \\ \hline 6\ 5 \end{array} \qquad \begin{array}{r} 42 \\ +23 \\ \hline 65 \end{array}$$

B

55	34	22	71	63	15
+41	+34	+36	+27	+14	+83
96	68	58	98	77	98

46	67	23	49	20	32
+53	+22	+62	+10	+76	+55
99	89	85	59	96	87

30	11	37	44	17	19
+62	+88	+40	+54	+12	+80
92	99	77	98	29	99

SUBTRACTING TWO-PLACE NUMBERS

A

First subtract the ones.
Then subtract the tens.

tens ones
$$\begin{array}{r} 5\ 6 \\ -2\ 3 \\ \hline 3\ 3 \end{array} \qquad \begin{array}{r} 56 \\ -23 \\ \hline 33 \end{array}$$

B

48	36	87	56	54	75
−35	−12	−53	−50	−21	−34
13	24	34	6	33	41

47	77	95	99	18	87
−36	−25	−90	−46	−14	−45
11	52	5	53	4	42

C

$$\left. \begin{array}{r} 76 \\ -23 \\ \hline 53 \\ 76 \end{array} \right\} \begin{array}{l} \text{Add these} \\ \text{to check} \\ \text{Same as top} \\ \text{number} \end{array}$$

$$\left. \begin{array}{r} 54 \\ -21 \\ \hline 33 \\ 54 \end{array} \right\} \begin{array}{l} \text{Add} \\ \text{to check} \end{array}$$

$$\left. \begin{array}{r} 75 \\ -34 \\ \hline 41 \\ 75 \end{array} \right\} \begin{array}{l} \text{Add} \\ \text{to check} \end{array}$$

LESSON 44. Nickels and Dimes

Purpose: To add nickels and dimes and express the values in cents.
Group Activity
Materials: dual board, number markers 1 to 9 and 0, five 5-blocks, each with a nickel taped on it, five 10-blocks, each with a dime taped on it
- A child places 1 nickel (on a block) in the ones compartment and records it with number marker 5.
- On the chalkboard write 1 nickel = 5¢.
- A child adds 1 nickel and moves both to the tens compartment and records them with markers for 10.
- A child adds a third nickel by putting it in the ones compartment and records the total with markers for 15.
- Build and record 2 dimes (20); then add 1 nickel (25).

Mystery Coins
Materials: blocks with coins (from previous activity), box or scarf
- While the children's eyes are closed, hide 5 nickels (on blocks).
- Say, "Open your eyes. The coins under this box are worth 25 cents." (Write the mystery amount on a card to help visual learners.)
- Children guess the coins and lift the box to check.

Workbook Page: Go over the illustrations. The children finish the page independently.

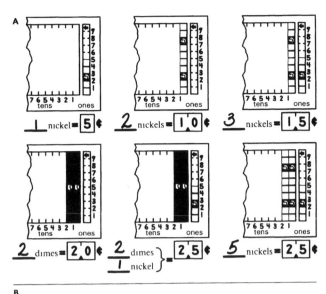

NICKELS AND DIMES

LESSON 45. Dimes and Dollars

Purpose: To learn the relationship between pennies, dimes, and dollars.
Note: These experiments are an excellent foundation for understanding percent.
Group Activity
Finding Values in the Dual Board
Materials: dual board, 100 cubes, picture of dollar bill, 10-blocks
- Display cubes (with pennies on some of them) and explain that just as the 1 cubes are the ones of the number system, so the pennies are the ones in our money system.
- A child fills the tens compartment of the dual board with rows of cubes (10 rows of 10 cubes each).
- Let them count to verify the total of 100 cubes.
- Show a picture of a dollar bill and elicit that it is equal in value to 100 pennies.
- On the chalkboard write $1.00 = 100 pennies.
- Show that 10 dimes equal 1 dollar in value by covering each row of 10 cubes with a 10-block with a dime on it.
- On the chalkboard write $1.00 = 10 dimes.
- Write values in cents: 1 dime = 10¢, 2 dimes = 20¢, ... 10 dimes = 100¢.

Coin Lotto (see p. 43).
Workbook Page: Go over the illustrations. The children finish the page independently.

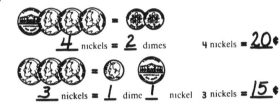

DIMES AND DOLLARS

LESSON 46. Nickels, Dimes, and Dollars

Purpose: To learn about the relationship of nickels to dimes and each to one dollar; to record the values in cents.

Group Activity

Finding Values in the Number Track

Materials: number track 1 to 100, ten 10-blocks (with a dime on each), ten 5-blocks (with a nickel on each), ten cubes (with a penny on each)

- Place the ten cubes in the first decade of the number track; elicit that the whole track would hold 100 pennies.
- On the board write 1 dollar = 100¢ and $1.00 = 100¢.
- In the number track show that 10 dimes (on blocks) equal 100¢.
- Elicit that 10 nickels equal 50¢ (demonstrate).
- Write on the board 5 dimes = 50¢ and 10 nickels = 50¢.

Hiding Game in the Number Track

Materials: number track, blocks with coins, scarf

- Place groups of blocks with coins in the number track.
- Cover the blocks with a scarf, but let the last number (the total) show (perhaps 50).
- The child who can name all the hidden coins correctly may hide the next group of coins in the number track.

Workbook Page: Go over the relationships pictured. The children finish the page independently.

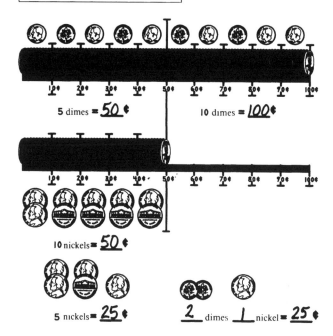

NICKELS, DIMES, AND DOLLARS

1 dollar = _100_ ¢
$1.00 = _100_ ¢
1 dollar = _10_ dimes

5 dimes = _50_ ¢   10 dimes = _100_ ¢

10 nickels = _50_ ¢

5 nickels = _25_ ¢   _2_ dimes _1_ nickel = _25_ ¢

LESSON 47. Quarters and Half-Dollars

Purpose: To learn the relationship of half-dollars and quarters to dollars and to pennies, dimes, and nickels.

Group Activity

Materials: number track 1 to 100, number blocks with coins, 5 index cards (one with a picture of a half-dollar and four with a quarter), pencil

- Divide the track into two equal parts by placing a pencil at 50, the halfway mark, and write 50 + 50 = 100 on the chalkboard.
- Stand the card with the picture of a half-dollar in front of the first half of the track, 1 to 50.
- Have the children show the coins (on blocks) that measure 50: 5 dimes or 10 nickels. Elicit that 50 pennies make 50¢.
- Show the four parts (quarters) of the track: put a card with a quarter at 25, one at 50, one at 75, and one at 100. The four parts are now visible.
- Put 2 ten-blocks and a 5-block in the track; elicit that 25 is one-quarter of the track. Point to the card with a quarter.
- Have children add groups of 2 tens and a 5 in the track to show the value of 2 quarters, 3 quarters, and 4 quarters.

Mystery Coins (see Lesson 44) **or Coin Lotto** (see p. 43)

Workbook Page: Go over the relationships. The children finish the page independently.

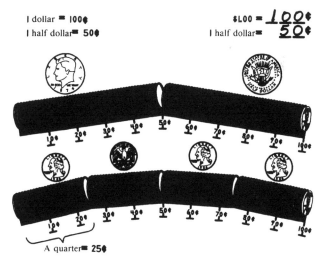

QUARTERS AND HALF DOLLARS

1 dollar = 100¢ $1.00 = _100_ ¢
1 half dollar = 50¢   1 half dollar = _50_ ¢

A quarter = 25¢

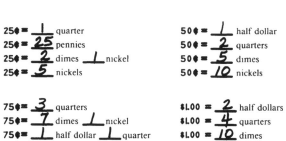

25¢ = _1_ quarter   50¢ = _1_ half dollar
25¢ = _25_ pennies   50¢ = _2_ quarters
25¢ = _2_ dimes _1_ nickel   50¢ = _5_ dimes
25¢ = _5_ nickels   50¢ = _10_ nickels

75¢ = _3_ quarters $1.00 = _2_ half dollars
75¢ = _7_ dimes _1_ nickel $1.00 = _4_ quarters
75¢ = _1_ half dollar _1_ quarter $1.00 = _10_ dimes

LESSON 48. Test

Purpose: To test knowledge of adding or subtracting 10 from 2-place numbers and adding or subtracting 2-place numbers.

Group Activity

Materials: chalkboard
- On the chalkboard write +10 and −10.
- Call on a child to dictate a 2-place number such as 45, and write it on the chalkboard.
- Point to +10 (child answers, "55"), point to +10 again ("65"), point to −10 ("55"), and so on.
- Children enjoy showing their agility in this game as you switch back and forth between +10 and −10.
- Review the addition and subtraction of two 2-place numbers in column form.
- Remind children that they start with ones and then work with tens.

Workbook Page: A. Go over a few examples orally.
B. Point out that there are addition and subtraction examples.
C. Go over the problems of finding how much more.
The children finish the page independently.

TEST

A

54 + 10 = **64**   18 − 10 = **8**
10 + 46 = **56**   87 − 10 = **77**
65 + 10 = **75**   96 − 10 = **86**
10 + 44 = **54**   43 − 20 = **23**
72 + 10 = **82**   34 − 10 = **24**
67 + 10 = **77**   92 − 10 = **82**
10 + 55 = **65**   25 − 20 = **5**

B

28	60	10		49	51	83
+10	+24	+63		−20	−10	−10
38	**84**	**73**		**29**	**41**	**73**

C

The book costs **$1.00**.
Tom has only **70¢**.
   How much more money does Tom need to buy the book?

|100| − |70| = |30|

Tom needs **30**¢ more.

Mario had **$1.00**.
He got a toy for **80¢**.
   How much money did he have left?

|100| − |80| = |20|

Mario had **20**¢ left.

UNIT 8. TRANSFER TO HIGHER DECADES

Lessons in this unit:
49. Addition within the Decades
50. Subtraction within the Decades
51. Completing Decades
52. Subtracting from Full Decades
53. Combinations That Make 20

Transfer to Higher Decades

In this unit children learn to move up or down the number track from 1 to 100 with ease. A child places two blocks, such as 4 + 5, in the first section of the track. Now the teacher moves both blocks decade by decade through the entire track. The pupils realize that 4 + 5 = 9 holds true in any decade.

$$4 + 5 = 9$$
$$14 + 5 = 19$$
$$24 + 5 = 29$$

Thus, the children are learning how to transfer an addition fact within a decade (4 + 5) to a higher decade. They discover that they can do the same with a basic subtraction fact such as 6 − 5 = 1.

Mental Arithmetic

In lessons 51 and 52 children learn to complete decades and to subtract from full decades; this means they are dealing with the basic number facts with a sum of 10. When children transfer a fact like 4 + 6 = 10 to higher decades, they are each time completing a decade. They may think, "14 needs what to make 20?" (6) or "24 needs what to make 30?" (6), and see that they are completing each decade. They do this in their heads without carrying 1 ten.

In subtracting from full decades they learn to subtract without the cumbersome process of borrowing 1 ten, or regrouping. They know that 10 − 6 = 4 and see that 30 − 6 = 24 and 20 − 6 = 14. We call this subtracting from full decades. It will be used later in learning the 9-table in multiplication.

Once again, the ability to do addition in one's head is made easier. Here is how this ability is used in adding long columns of numbers. The partial sums may be 6 + 7 (13) + 7 (20) + 4 (24) + 6 (30). A decade is completed at every other step.

The Associative Property of Addition

Many teachers want their pupils to be familiar with the concepts and vocabulary that were introduced with the New Math approach and that still appear in many workbooks.

Once students understand how to transfer a basic fact to a higher decade, they can take a fact such as 3 + 5 and place it in another decade (43 + 5). They recognize that 3 and 5 still "associate" with each other and reach 8, but this time in the 40s.

$$
\begin{aligned}
43 + 5 &= (40 + 3) + 5 \quad \text{expanded form of 43} \\
&= 40 + (3 + 5) \quad \text{the associative} \\
&\qquad\qquad\qquad\quad \text{property of addition} \\
&= 40 + 8 \quad\quad\quad\; \text{renaming 3 + 5 as 8} \\
&= 48
\end{aligned}
$$

Working with the Structural Arithmetic materials teaches children to add 43 + 5 by visualizing the decade of the 40s, in which the 3- and 5-blocks are added, or "associated," to give 48. Their experiences with the materials enable them to understand this complicated vocabulary.

In this unit each group of facts is studied separately, and therefore children master the facts with full insight.

The concepts in this unit are not tested until the end of Unit 9.

GAMES AND DEMONSTRATIONS

Stop-and-Go Game (use with Lesson 49)
Materials: number track 1 to 60, five 10-blocks for each team, number blocks, stop-and-go cube

- Divide the class into teams A and B.
- Team A chooses a combination, perhaps 4 + 5, and places it in the track. Team B places its combination alongside the track.
* Say to Team A, "You are adding 4 + 5. Drop the stop-and-go cube. If you get Go, you can move your combination up to the next decade."
- If player A gets Go, she pushes 4 + 5 up by inserting a 10-block before them and says, "14 and 5 are 19! I'm on 19 now!"
- Player B tosses the stop-and-go cube next and pushes his combination up with a 10-block.
- Any team throwing Stop gets no turn. (If a team throws Stop three times in a row, it can be given a free turn.)
- The first team to arrive in the 60s wins. (Team A will finish with 64 + 5 = 69.)
- You may want to appoint a scribe for each team who will write each higher-decade fact on the chalkboard under the team's name.

LESSON 49. Addition within the Decades

Purpose: To discover that any basic addition fact can be transferred to higher decades.
Group Activity
Materials: number track, number blocks, 10-blocks

- Give each child one or two sections of the number track.
- Put the track together by asking, "Who has the first section?, Who has the teens?, What comes after the teens?" and so forth.
- When the track is assembled, insert a combination of blocks in the first section, perhaps 4 and 5.
- Ask a child to move the combination to the second decade and insert a 10-block in the first decade.
- Elicit that 14 + 5 = 19 and ask a child to write it on the board.
- Have children take turns moving the combination up through each decade to 94 + 5 = 99.

Stop-and-Go Game—Using the Number Track (see top of this page)
Workbook Page: Go over the illustration. The children finish the page independently, writing facts of their own choosing in higher decades.

ADDITION WITHIN THE DECADES

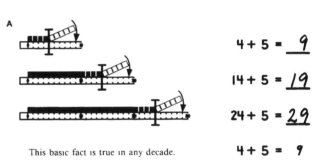

4 + 5 = 9
14 + 5 = 19
24 + 5 = 29

This basic fact is true in any decade.   4 + 5 = 9

B Write each basic fact in higher decades.

| 4 + 3 = 7 | | 6 + 3 = 9 |
| 24 + 3 = 27 | | |

| 3 + 5 = 8 | | 5 + 2 = 7 |

Answers will vary.

LESSON 50. Subtraction within the Decades

Purpose: To discover that any basic subtraction fact can be transferred to higher decades.

Group Activity

Materials: number track, number blocks, 10-blocks
- Put two blocks that total 6, such as 1 and 5 in the first decade of the number track.
- Ask a child to demonstrate 6 − 5 = 1 with the blocks.
- Have a child push this combination into the next decade by inserting a 10-block in the first decade.
- Demonstrate 16 − 5 = 11 and then 26 − 5 = 21.
- Call on children to write the equations on the board.
- Continue to the final decade, 96 − 5 = 91.

Scarf Game

Materials: number track, number blocks, 10-blocks, long scarf
- In the first section of the track place blocks for a subtraction fact, such as 6 − 5 = 1. Cover the track with a scarf.
- Child after child states the fact in successively higher decades as you insert a new 10-block each time to push the combination up.
- Stop at 56. Ask, "What is left under the scarf when I subtract 5?" (remove the 5-block).
- Remove the scarf for the children to check (51).

Workbook Page: Go over the page. The children finish the page independently.

SUBTRACTION WITHIN THE DECADES

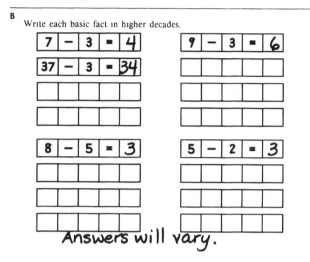

This basic fact is true in any decade.

6 − 5 = 1
16 − 5 = 11
26 − 5 = 21
6 − 5 = 1

Write each basic fact in higher decades.

| 7 − 3 = 4 | | 9 − 3 = 6 |
| 37 − 3 = 34 | | |

| 8 − 5 = 3 | | 5 − 2 = 3 |

Answers will vary.

LESSON 51. Completing Decades

Purpose: To discover that the combinations that make 10 can be transferred to higher decades.

Group Activity

Materials: number track, ten 10-blocks, 10-box filled with blocks
- In the track, build 26 (2 tens and a 6-block).
- Ask, "What does 26 need to reach 30?"
- A child inserts the 4-block, states the fact, and writes the equation on the chalkboard: 26 + 4 = 30.
- Now give each child a block from 1 to 10.
- Keep blocks 1 to 9 for your part in the activity.
- Put 7 in the track. Ask, "7 needs what to make 10?"
- The child with the 3-block puts it in the track and says, "7 + 3 = 10."
- Ask a similar question for the next decade, "16 needs what to make 20?" (4). Leave the blocks in the track.
- Continue by asking for a different combination to fill each decade of the track: 23 + __ = 30, 34 + __ = 40, 45 + __ = 50, 51 + __ = 60, and so on.
- Put all the blocks back in the 10-box when finished.

Workbook Page: Go over the illustration. The children finish the page independently.

COMPLETING DECADES

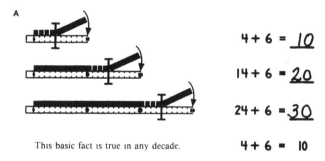

This basic fact is true in any decade.

4 + 6 = 10
14 + 6 = 20
24 + 6 = 30
4 + 6 = 10

Write each basic fact in higher decades.

| 5 + 5 = 10 | | 6 + 4 = 10 |
| 15 + 5 = 20 | | |

| 3 + 7 = 10 | | 8 + 2 = 10 |

Answers will vary.

LESSON 52. Subtracting from Full Decades

Purpose: To discover that the facts that result from subtracting numbers from 10 can be transferred to higher decades.
Note: The ability to subtract a number from a full decade will help children master the 9-table quickly when they study multiplication.

Group Activity
Materials: number track, number blocks, 10-blocks
- Fill each decade of the number track with a different combination that makes 10 (see Lesson 51).
- Ask a child to state the addition fact in the final decade; perhaps it is 91 + 9 = 100.
- Say, "Show us the related subtraction fact."
- She subtracts the 9-block and says, "100 − 9 = 91."
- Another child writes this fact on the chalkboard (remove blocks from the final decade).
- The next child looks at the blocks in the next to last decade, demonstrates the subtraction fact 90 − 7 = 83, and writes the equation on the board.
- The children take turns until they have emptied the track and have written ten subtraction facts.

Workbook Page: Go over the illustrations. The children finish the page independently.

SUBTRACTING FROM FULL DECADES

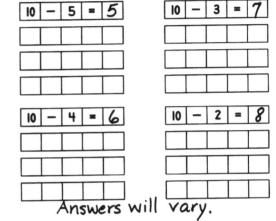

This basic fact is true in any decade.

10 − 6 = 4

Write each basic fact in higher decades.

Answers will vary.

LESSON 53. Combinations That Make 20

Purpose: To learn that the combinations that make 10 when transferred to the teens become combinations that make 20.

Group Activity
Materials: 20-tray, two sets of number blocks 1 to 10, ten 10-blocks
- Children take turns building the stair from 1 to 20.
- Scatter the other set of blocks 1 to 10 on the table.
- Point to 19; ask, "What does 19 need to make 20?" (1).
- A child adds the 1-block and says, "19 + 1 = 20."
- Do all combinations up to "11 + 9 = 20."
- Elicit that these are the 10-facts "one-flight up."
- Hide two blocks that make 20, perhaps 19 and 1.
- Say, "I have hidden 20 in all. If I take 1 away (do so), what is left?" (19). Elicit, "20 − 1 = 19."

Workbook Page: A. Go over the examples.
B. Place blocks for 15¢ and 5¢ in the number track. Say, "The pen cost 15¢. The clerk keeps 15¢ by subtracting it from your 20¢. The clerk gives you back the change (5¢)." The children finish the page independently.

COMBINATIONS THAT MAKE 20

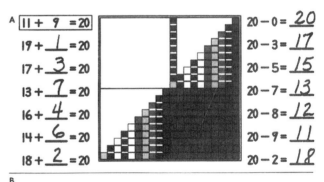

How Much Change?

Rob has **2** dimes.
A pen costs **15¢**.
How much change will Rob get back?

$20 - 15 = 5$
5 ¢ change

Think:
Cross off the 15¢ Rob spent.
The change is left.

Stella has **2** dimes.
She spent **19¢**.
How much change will she get back?

$20 - 19 = 1$
Stella will get **1** ¢ change.

Alberto has **50¢**.
He spent **40¢** for dog food.
How much change will he get?

$50 - 40 = 10$
Alberto will get **10** ¢ change.

UNIT 9. TEEN FACTS

Lessons in this unit:
54. Adding to 9 in the 20-Tray
55. Adding to 9 in the Number Track
56. Adding to 8 in the Number Track
57. Test

In Units 6, 7, and 8, children reviewed the basic addition and subtraction facts and discovered that they could be transferred to solve addition and subtraction facts in the higher decades. Children are now ready to deal with facts that cross the boundary line of 10; there will be 36 new addition facts and 36 new subtraction facts (see charts, pp. 89 and 90).

Bridging from One Decade into Another

Up to this point the central role played by 10 has been emphasized. No fact has extended beyond 10, that is, from one decade into the next decade. For instance, children have added 6 to 1, 2, 3, and 4, but not to 5. The combination $5 + 6$ extends beyond the first decade of the number track. The 6-block forms a bridge that goes from 5 in the first decade to 11 in the next decade, thus crossing the 10-line.

Correspondingly, $35 + 6$ crosses beyond the 30s and into the decade of the 40s. In this case the 6 forms a bridge that reaches from a number in one decade (35) to a number in the next decade (41). Hence, the addition facts such as $5 + 6$ or $9 + 2$ can be called "bridging facts." Since most teachers are unfamiliar with this concept of bridging, we have decided to call them "teen facts."

Mental Computation in Column Addition

The teen facts are the most difficult facts children have to learn. Yet they need to know these addition facts in order to add columns of figures. In the previous units they learned to keep successive decades in mind, to add within a decade, and to complete decades. Now they must remember the facts that cross from one decade into the next. For example, $9 + 9 + 8 + 7$ gives the following partial sums to be added mentally: $9 + 9$ (18) $+ 8$ (26) $+ 7$ (33).

The basic teen facts involved are $9 + 9 = 18$, $8 + 8 = 16$, and $6 + 7 = 13$, but they are being added mentally in higher decades. As children go from figure to figure, they bridge from decade to decade.

Mental Computation in Subtraction Examples

Subtraction examples with 2-place or 3-place numbers in written form provide new challenges. First, it is difficult for some children to understand the concept of regrouping, or borrowing 1 ten, unless it is explained with adequate materials. And second, teachers seldom realize that after 1 ten has been borrowed, or regrouped into the ones column, all the subtracting is from teen numbers.

Children with poor rote memories often do not know the subtraction facts and find it very difficult to count them out accurately. In the next units, five proven techniques are presented to help children master teen facts in both addition and subtraction (see charts p. 89 and p. 90).

Adding to 9; Adding to 8

In Unit 9 children begin the study of teen facts with the techniques of adding to 9 and adding to 8. Together these give them the key to the mastery of 15 addition facts and 15 subtraction facts. This results in a great economy in learning since one generalization enables children to master as many as eight facts at once. Many children doing remedial work can deal with adding to 9 only by laboriously counting out dots to solve the combination; they are excited to find there is an easier way to learn the facts. With the materials they discover the generalization that adding a number to 9 gives a sum 1 less than if the same number had been added to 10. Thus, $9 + 8 = 17$.

Higher-Decade Facts

In the workbook, children transfer each teen fact to higher decades instead of being drilled on the same fact over and over again. It gives them a sense of accomplishment to be able to create new facts of their own choosing. For example, they might transfer $9 + 8 = 17$ to these decades: $49 + 8 = 57$ and $89 + 8 = 97$.

GAMES AND DEMONSTRATIONS

Adding to 10 (use with Lesson 54)
Materials: 20-tray, two sets of number blocks 1 to 10, ten 10-blocks
- Have the children build the 20-stair in the 20-tray.
* Ask, "What is 10 and 5?" (15), "10 and 8?" (18), and so on.
- Children take turns selecting a teen combination and stating the fact, perhaps "10 + 7 = 17."
- Each child keeps the two blocks for the next game.
- The stair 1 to 10 remains in place.

Calling Back Game—The Stair in Reverse
Materials: same as above
- Each child has two blocks that make a teen number.
- Ask for blocks so as to build the stair in reverse.
- Ask, "Who has 20?" Place it as the last step in the 20-tray.
- Ask, "Who has the number just before 20?" (19).
- Ask, "Who has the number before 19?" "Before 18?" until the entire stair 1 to 20 is complete.
- Call on a child to descend the stair with a finger and name each step (20, 19, 18 . . .). This prepares students for the adding-to-9 facts (see below).

Adding to 9 (use with Lesson 54)
Materials: 20-tray, two sets of number blocks 1 to 10, ten 10-blocks, an extra 9-block
- Build the stair 1 to 20 in the 20-tray.
- Point to step 15. Ask, "What is 10 plus 5?" (15).
- Remove the 10-block and replace it with the 9-block.
- Hold the 5-block in place, leaving a gap of 1 unit above the 9-block.
- Call on a child to put a finger into this gap.
- Now ask the child to lower the 5-block so it touches the 9-block.
* Say, "Think! What happens when you add 5 to 9?" (you go down one).
- Ask, "9 and 5 is only . . . ?" (14).
- Shift the 9-block so it takes the place of the 10-block in a different number, perhaps 13.
- This time a child says, "10 + 3 is 13, but 9 + 3 is only 12," as he pushes the 3-block down.
- Children take turns adding each number block to 9, thus covering all the facts: 9 + 2 = 11, 9 + 3 = 12, 9 + 4 = 13, 9 + 5 = 14, 9 + 6 = 15, 9 + 7 = 16, 9 + 8 = 17, 9 + 9 = 18.

LESSON 54. Adding to 9 in the 20-Tray

Purpose: To learn that when a number is added to 9, the sum is 1 less than when the same number is added to 10.
Group Activity
Adding to 10 (see p. 56)
Calling Back Game (see p. 56)
Adding to 9 (see p. 56)
Snake Game—Adding to 9 (see p. 8)
Materials: number blocks 1 to 10, ten 9-blocks, ten index cards labeled with numbers 11 to 20
- Divide the group into two teams.
- Turn the cards facedown.
- Scatter all the blocks on the table.
- The first player selects a card, perhaps 15.
- She forms a combination of two blocks whose sum is 15. (A rule for this game is that one addend must be 9; the other will therefore be 6.)
- The child adds blocks 9 and 6 to her team's snake.
- The team with the longer snake wins.

Workbook Page: **A.** Go over the illustration.
B and **C.** On the chalkboard write examples, making each number that is added to 9 dark. Point to 9 + 7. Say, "Not 17, but . . . ?" (16). Go over the examples orally first. The children finish the page independently.

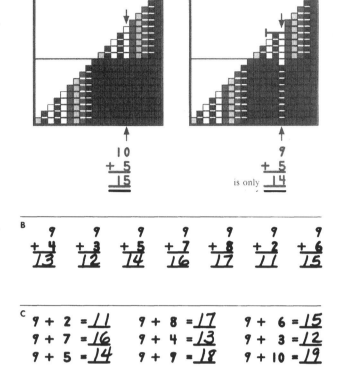

ADDING TO 9 IN THE 20-TRAY

A. Adding to 10 — Adding to 9

10 + 5 = 15   9 + 5 is only 14

B.
9 + 4 = 13   9 + 3 = 12   9 + 5 = 14   9 + 7 = 16   9 + 8 = 17   9 + 2 = 11   9 + 6 = 15

C.
9 + 2 = 11   9 + 8 = 17   9 + 6 = 15
9 + 7 = 16   9 + 4 = 13   9 + 3 = 12
9 + 5 = 14   9 + 9 = 18   9 + 10 = 19

LESSON 55. Adding to 9 in the Number Track

Purpose: To discover the facts of adding to 9 in the number track and to transfer them to higher decades.
Group Activity
Materials: number track 1 to 50, two sets of number blocks 1 to 10
- Place a 10-block in the track and add a 4-block to it.
- Ask, "10 and 4 are . . . ?" (14).
- Replace the 10-block with a 9-block; leave the 4-block in place.
- Ask, "9 and 4 are . . . ?" and call on a child to push the 4-block down to fill the gap (13).
- Move this combination to higher decades; place a 10-block in the first decade each time: 19 + 4, 29 + 4, etc.

Speed Drop
Note: Children say the answer before the block drops.
Materials: same as above
- Place a 9-block in the track; hold a 4-block above the track.
- Say, "9 and 4 are . . . ?" as your hand descends slowly with the 4-block.
- If the child says, "13" before the block lands, he may "keep" the 4-block as a prize.

Workbook Page: **A** and **B.** Go over the illustrations. The children finish the page independently.

ADDING TO 9 IN THE NUMBER TRACK

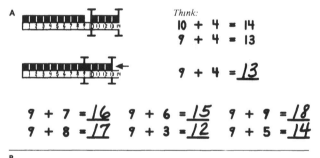

A. Think:
10 + 4 = 14
9 + 4 = 13

9 + 4 = 13

9 + 7 = 16   9 + 6 = 15   9 + 9 = 18
9 + 8 = 17   9 + 3 = 12   9 + 5 = 14

B. Higher Decade Facts

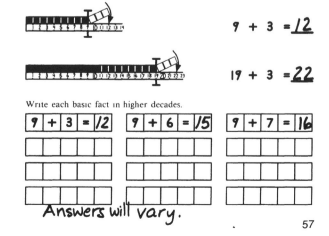

9 + 3 = 12

19 + 3 = 22

Write each basic fact in higher decades.

| 9 | + | 3 | = | 12 | | 9 | + | 6 | = | 15 | | 9 | + | 7 | = | 16 |

Answers will vary.

LESSON 56. Adding to 8 in the Number Track

Purpose: To learn that when a number is added to 8, the sum is 2 less than when the same number is added to 10.

Group Activity

Note: The number that is 2 down from an even number is the next lower even number (10, 8, 6, 4, 2). The number that is 2 down from an odd number is the next lower odd number (9, 7, 5, 3, 1).

Materials: number track 1 to 50, two sets of number blocks 1 to 10

- Put blocks 10 and 4 in the track and ask, "10 and 4 are . . . ?"
- Replace the 10-block with an 8-block.
- Ask, "8 and 4 are . . . ?" Have a child push the 4-block down 2 units to meet the 8-block and give the sum.
- Move the combination to higher decades, 18 + 4, 28 + 4, and 38 + 4.

Speed Drop Variation (see Lesson 55)

Materials: number track 1 to 50, two sets of number blocks 1 to 10

- Construct the stair of even numbers on the table: 2, 4, 6, 8.
- To the 8-block in the track add one even number after another, each time pointing out that the answer contains the next lower even number.
- Ask "8 + 8 = ?" (16), "8 + 6 = ?" (14), "8 + 4 = ?" (12).
- Do the same with the stair of odd numbers: 8 + 9 = ?" (17), "8 + 7 = ?" (15), "8 + 5 = ?" (13), "8 + 3 = ?" (11).

Workbook Page: The children finish the page independently.

LESSON 57. Test

Purpose: To test mastery of the following groups of facts: completion of decades, adding to 9, adding to 8, and the related higher-decade facts.

Group Activity

Review: For Adding to 9
- Give children practice naming the number 1 down from a number. Say, "8"; a child responds, "7."
- Children write numbers in sequence from 20 to 1.

Review: For Adding to 8
- Give children practice naming the number 2 down from a number. Say, "8"; a child responds, "6."
- Children write the even numbers in reverse order: 20, 18, 16 . . . 2; then the odd numbers, 19, 17, 15 . . . 1.

Stop-and-Go Game

Materials: index cards with examples of adding to 8 and adding to 9, stop-and-go cube

- Turn the cards facedown.
- The players from teams A and B take turns dropping the stop-and-go cube.
- If the cube lands on Go, the player turns up a card and writes the example below her team's name.

Workbook Page: Go over the test orally if necessary. The children complete the page independently.

ADDING TO 8 IN THE NUMBER TRACK

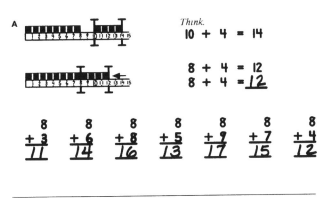

A

Think.
10 + 4 = 14

8 + 4 = 12
8 + 4 = 12

8+3=11 8+6=14 8+8=16 8+5=13 8+9=17 8+7=15 8+4=12

B Higher Decade Facts

18 + 4 = 22

Write each basic fact in higher decades.

| 8 + 4 = 12 | 8 + 7 = 15 | 8 + 5 = 13 |

Answers will vary.

TEST

A 5 + 5 = 10   7 + 3 = 10   6 + 4 = 10
   65 + 5 = 70 87 + 3 = 90 26 + 4 = 30
   75 + 5 = 80 57 + 3 = 60 16 + 4 = 20

B 9+4=13 9+5=14 9+8=17 9+9=18 9+7=16 9+2=11 9+6=15

C 9 + 3 = 12   9 + 8 = 17   9 + 6 = 15
   29 + 3 = 32 49 + 8 = 57 39 + 6 = 45
   19 + 3 = 22 59 + 8 = 67 79 + 6 = 85
   69 + 3 = 72 19 + 8 = 27 89 + 6 = 95

D 8+3=11 8+5=13 8+7=15 8+9=17 8+4=12 8+6=14 8+8=16

   8+7=15 9+6=15 8+3=11 9+9=18 8+5=13 9+7=16 8+4=12

UNIT 10. TELLING TIME

Lessons in this unit:
58. What Hour Is It?
59. Quarters and Halves of an Hour
60. Minutes After the Hour
61. Minutes Before the Hour
62. What Time Is It?

The Clock Face

Many children today read their digital watches and can name the numbers shown, reading 12:55 as "twelve fifty-five," but cannot tell time in the old-fashioned sense of being able to read a clock face. Moreover, even when children can tell time on a clock face, it does not mean they understand the relationship between the hour hand and the minute hand.

The Relationship between the Hands

In order to learn about hours and minutes, it is important for children to understand the relationship between the movements of the two hands. To do this the children should work with model clocks in which the two hands are geared together or with an old alarm clock from which the glass has been removed.

Set the model clock before the group and identify each hand. You may want to make the minute hand a different color from the hour hand. Start by putting both hands of the clock at 12. Move the minute hand slowly in a clockwise direction. Elicit that the hour hand also moves although no one is touching it.

Show that the minute hand is counting minute after minute; it will count 60 minutes by going around the circle one full time. Stop when the minute hand reaches 12. Elicit that the hour hand has traveled a very short distance and now points to 1. This tells us that one hour has been counted out.

Naming the Hours of the Clock

Next, call on a child to demonstrate the second full hour. Let the child move the minute hand through one complete circle and stop at 12. Elicit that the hour hand now points to 2 and tells us that two hours have been counted. We say, "It is 2 o'clock." Call on a child to demonstrate another full circle of the minute hand and tell what the hour hand does (it moves to 3). We call this "3 o'clock." Give different children a chance to move the minute hand one full hour and tell the time the clock shows.

The Clock Face and Its 5-Minute Periods

The two hands of the clock each tell a different story, but they do so using the same numbers. Thus the children must first learn the location on the circle of each number from 1 to 12. Only then can they name the different story each hand is recording.

The minute hand points to minute after minute around the face of the clock, but for convenience' sake we think in 5-minute periods. We give the end of each period its own name: 5 after, 10 after, 15 after, 20 after, and 25 after, until half-past. From then on we concentrate on measuring the distance in minutes that the minute hand must travel to complete the hour. We say 25 minutes of or to the next hour. We stop when the minute hand has completed the circle.

How To Make a Clock Face (for games, p. 60)

Take two manila folders of different colors. To represent the right half of the clock, stretch one folder lengthwise. Trace six 5-blocks in a semicircle, three for each quarter (see Lesson 60 in the workbook). At the end of each 5-minute period, draw a square to hold a number marker.

Complete the clock face by stretching out the other folder and placing it on the left side. Trace a similar pattern of 5-blocks on the left folder. Label the right half "after" and the left half "of." Position a toy house at the top of the circle. Cut out a minute hand to point to the minutes. The quarters of the circle are visibly marked by the folds and will be introduced in Lesson 59.

Clock Games (see p. 60)

Many games can be played on this cardboard clock face. Children can begin by measuring the 5-minute periods using 5-blocks. Once they have done this they are ready to traverse the circle with a toy animal or cube.

The Positions of the Markers (use before Lesson 58)
Materials: number markers 1 to 10 and the markers for the plus and minus signs covered with labels for 11 and 12

Have the children put each number in place in succession around the clock face. They are now ready to carry out the activities in Lessons 58 through 61.

GAMES AND DEMONSTRATIONS

Stop-and-Go Game (use after Lesson 61)
Note: Before the children play this game, they must thoroughly understand the work in Lessons 58 to 61.
Materials: cardboard clock face, number markers 1 to 12, twelve 5-blocks, stop-and-go cube

- Go over the rules for playing Stop and Go (p. 37)
- Each child on a team selects its specially colored cube and places it at the house (home).
- The children put numbers 1 to 12 in place.
- A player tosses the stop-and-go cube, puts one 5-block in place, says, "5 after," and moves his cube to rest on top of the number marker for 1.
- Player B gets Stop and forfeits the turn.
* Player A tosses the stop-and-go cube again.
- Say, "You got Go! Put in another 5-block. Now move your marker to the next number" (2).
- The child announces, "Now I'm on 10 after."
- Whoever reaches half-past announces it and puts in six 5-blocks between 6 and 12, which will help the players measure the time "to the hour" (25 minutes of, 20 minutes of, . . . 5 minutes of).
- The player who gets the next Go removes the 5-block between 6 and 7 and says, "I'm on 25 of" (or "25 minutes to").
- Continue until one team reaches home.

Note: Children love to play a Parade Game in which each has a toy animal that marches from 1 to 12 side by side.

Domino Games (use after Lesson 61)
Materials: cardboard clock face, number markers 1 to 12, colored cubes for each team, dominoes with labels pasted on them: 5 after, 10 after, 15 after, 20 after, 25 after, half-past, 25 minutes of, 20 of, 15 of, 10 of, 5 of, a quarter past, a quarter of, and on the hour

The Basic Game
- Have children put the number markers in place.
- Turn the dominoes face down.
* Call on a child; say, "Turn up a domino!"
- The child does so and says, "25 after! It goes here!" (places the domino at the proper place).
- Play until all dominoes are in place.

Capture Peaks
- Turn the dominoes facedown.
- Each team gets 10 cubes of one color.
- A player picks a domino (5 after), reads it, and puts a cube on the number (1). Each domino is returned to the pool, making it possible for each position to have more than one cube on it.
- At the end of the game, the top-most cube claims the tower of cubes below it for its team.

LESSON 58. What Hour Is It?

Purpose: To learn about full hours.
Group Activity
Materials: model clock with gears
- Set the minute hand and hour hand on 12.
- Move the minute hand one complete circle around to 12 so the hour hand points to 1.
- Ask a child to turn the minute hand another full circle, or hour.
- Elicit that the hour hand now points to 2.
- A child names the time, "2 o'clock."
- Ask a child to move the minute hand around until it shows 3 o'clock.
- Work with many different full hours until the children see how the hour hand works.
- Have children do work similar to the workbook page at the chalkboard.

Workbook Page: A. Go over the time orally first.
B. The children draw in each hour hand.

WHAT HOUR IS IT?

A The little hand tells the hour.
It is called the **hour hand**.

1 o'clock   12 o'clock noon   9 o'clock

6 o'clock   4 o'clock   3 o'clock

B Draw the hour hand on each clock.

3 o'clock   5 o'clock   10 o'clock

2 o'clock   8 o'clock   7 o'clock

LESSON 59. Quarters and Halves of an Hour

Purpose: To learn what time it is when the minute hand has completed a quarter of a full turn, half a turn, and three quarters of a turn.
Group Activity
Materials: model clock with gears
- Set the clock to show 4 o'clock.
- Ask a child to move the minute hand half way around the circle until it points to 6.
- Elicit that the hour hand traveled half the way between 4 and 5; we call this "half past 4."
- On the chalkboard draw a circle. Divide it into four quarters, shade in the first quarter, and draw a minute hand at a quarter past.
- Set the clock to show 5 o'clock.
- Have a child turn the clock hands to a quarter past the hour, then half past.
- Turn the minute hand slowly until it points to 9.
- Explain that since it has a quarter of the way to go, we call it "a quarter of."
- Ask where the hour hand is now.

Workbook Page: Go over the page. The children finish the page independently.

QUARTERS AND HALVES OF AN HOUR

The big hand is called the **minute hand**. It has gone **a quarter past** the hour. | a quarter past 7 (The little hand tells the hour.) | a quarter past 11

half past the hour | half past 7 | half past 11

a quarter of the hour | a quarter of 10 | a quarter of 12

on the hour | 3 o'clock | 12 o'clock

LESSON 60. Minutes After the Hour

Purpose: To learn to figure the number of minutes after the hour and to name each 5-minute period.
Group Activity
Materials: cardboard clock face with minute hand, toy house, six 5-blocks, number markers 1 to 6
- Review by recording different numbers of 5-blocks in the dual board up to six 5-blocks (see Lesson 44).
- Put the toy house at 12, where the trip will start.
- A child puts a 5-block on the circle and says, "1 five" and marks the distance with number 1.
- Show a cut-out minute hand traveling to 5 after.
- Say, "The minute hand points to 5 minutes after."
- A child adds another 5-block, places the number 2 at the end of 2 fives, and says, "10 after."
- Put in the third five and number 3; say, "15 after."
- Elicit that this is also called "a quarter past."
- The fourth and fifth blocks are labeled and named.
- The sixth five is labeled with number 6. We see that the hand has gone half way around to "half past."

Workbook Page: Go over the page. The children finish the page independently.

MINUTES AFTER THE HOUR

A

__5__ minutes after

__10__ minutes after

__15__ minutes after
a quarter past

__20__ minutes after

__25__ minutes after

half past

B Draw the minute hand.

5 minutes after

15 minutes after

10 minutes after

half past

25 minutes after

20 minutes after

LESSON 61. Minutes Before the Hour

Purpose: To learn to figure the number of minutes before the hour and to name each 5 minute period.
Group Activity
Materials: cardboard clock face with minute hand, six 5-blocks, number markers 1 to 12, toy house
- Put the numbers 1 to 6 in place.
- Put six 5-blocks around the left side of the clock from half past to the hour.
- Move the minute hand from half-past to the "25 of" mark. (Remove the 5-block between 6 and 7.)
- Say, "From now on we are interested in how far it is until we finish the hour and are 'home'."
- Count the 5s that measure the trip "home."
- A child counts, "5, 10, 15, 20, 25 minutes of."
- Move the hand up 5 minutes; remove the 5-block and elicit that there are now 20 minutes to go (20 of).
- Follow with 15 of, 10 of, 5 of, and the hour.

Stop-and-Go Game (see p. 60)
Domino Games (see p. 60)
Workbook Page: A and B. Go over the page orally first. The children finish the page independently.

MINUTES BEFORE THE HOUR

A

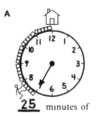
__25__ minutes of

__20__ minutes of

__15__ minutes of

__10__ minutes of

__5__ minutes of

the hour

B Draw the minute hand.

25 minutes of

15 minutes of

the hour

20 minutes of

5 minutes of

10 minutes of

LESSON 62. What Time Is It?

Purpose: To learn to read and understand time when it is written as on digital watches, transportation schedules, and television listings.

Materials: cardboard clock face with minute and hour hands, twelve 5-blocks, 12 cards labeled with a multiple of the 5 table: 5, 10, 15, 20, 25, 30, 35, 40, 45, 50, 55, 60

- Lay a 5-block on the clock face and place the card with 5 at the end of it.
- Continue by labeling the end of each added 5-block until you reach 60 (see workbook).
- On the chalkboard write the words *half-past 7*.
- Under that write 7:30. Elicit that this is the way we record time.
- Write "a quarter of 8" and show it with the clock hands.
- Have a child count out the nine 5-blocks and write 7:45.

Workbook Page: **A.** Go over the page orally first.
B. The children finish the page independently.

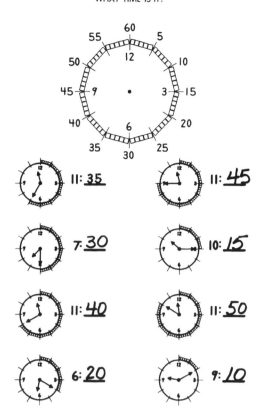

WHAT TIME IS IT?

UNIT 11. MORE TEEN FACTS

Lessons in this unit:
63. Adding 9 in the Number Track
64. Adding 8 in the Number Track
65. Subtracting 9 in the Number Track
66. Subtracting 8 in the Number Track
67. Test

Adding to 9

The children began their study of teen facts in Unit 9 by learning to add a number to 9 in the 20-stair. Then they transferred this technique to higher decades. In adding 6 to 49, for instance, they saw that 1 unit of the 6-block was used to reach 50, while 5 units extended into the next decade, yielding the higher-decade fact, 49 + 6 = 55.

Adding 9 to Numbers in the Number Track

In this unit the next group of facts is solved by the following technique: *adding 9 to a number*. In a demonstration the teacher places a block such as 3 in the number track, adds 10 to it, and then replaces the 10-block with a 9-block. Children see that 3 + 10 = 13 but 3 + 9 reaches only to 12, as one child put it, "Because 9 is 1 smaller than 10." This technique helps children master eight more facts with sums in the teens (see p. 89).

Higher-Decade Facts

The children know that in the higher decades, adding 10 to any number reaches the same ones place in the next higher decade. Now they will learn to add 9 to any number. They are encouraged to reason in two steps. To solve 37 + 9 = ___, they reason that 37 + 10 = 47, so 37 + 9 will be 46 (go down 1 in the next decade).

Adding 8 to Numbers

Adding 8 to a number is worked out with a technique similar to that of adding 9. Since 8 is 2 units less than 10, the sum will be 2 less than if 10 had been added to the number. For example, 37 + 10 = 47; 37 + 8 = 45. With this technique seven more teen facts can be solved (see the chart on p. 89).

Mental Computation

The examples in the higher decades are solved in equation form. This encourages pupils to find the answer in their own minds first and then to write it down. This helps them master "adding 9" in the higher decades. They will use this skill in column addition. In an example such as 7 + 8 + 9 + 7 + 6 + 9, there are two instances in which 9 is added to a 2-place number, 15 + 9 and 37 + 9. Once again they practice a skill by thinking up higher-decade facts of their own choosing at the end of the lesson.

Subtracting 9 in the Number Track

In experiments in the number track the children discover that when they subtract 9 from a teen number the answer is 1 more than if they had subtracted 10. The same technique is used to show subtracting 8 from teen numbers.

Written Computation

In subtracting 2-place and 3-place numbers from each other, the children must learn to borrow 1 from the denomination to the left. This gives them a teen number to subtract from each time. Thus the subtraction facts from teen numbers should be mastered before the children learn regrouping, or borrowing, in subtraction. The test for subtracting 8 and subtracting 9 from teen numbers is in Lesson 66.

GAMES AND DEMONSTRATIONS

Plus 10, Plus 9 (use with Lesson 63)
Materials: number track, colored cube for each of several teams, a die made by writing +10 on three sides of a cube and +9 on the other three sides, paper cup

- Each team starts by placing its cube on a different number in the first decade.
- The teams take turns tossing the die from the cup and moving their markers up the track by adding either 9 or 10 units.
- If Team A starts on 5, tosses the die, and gets +10, the player says, "5 + 10 = 15" and moves the markers to 15.
- After Team B moves, call on a player from Team A.
* Say, "You are on 15. Throw the die. What did you get?"
- The child says, "Plus 9! 15 plus 9 is only 24" (moves the marker to 24).
- The teams continue taking turns. The winner is the first one to reach a number in the 90s decade.

What Number Did I Hide? (use with Lesson 63)
Materials: number track 1 to 20, number blocks 1 to 10, a cardboard cover made to fit over the first section of the track

- Tell the children to close their eyes. Hide a block such as 3 under the cardboard cover.
* Say, "Open your eyes. I hid a block under here. Stick a 10-block in here to find out what it is."
- A child puts the 10-block in the second section of the track and pushes it down till it touches the hidden block.
- The child says, "It reaches 13, so the hidden block must be 3."
- Say, "Remove the 10-block." Ask, "What do you think will happen if you put in the 9-block? How far will it reach?"
- The child says, "3 plus 9 is 12, because 9 is 1 smaller than 10."
- Ask the child to check by adding the 9-block to 3.
- Continue giving the children turns figuring out which block you have hidden and then stating ahead of time the fact for adding 9 to your hidden number block.

GAMES AND DEMONSTRATIONS

Adding 9 in the Dual Board (use with Lesson 63)
Materials: dual board, ten 10-blocks, ten cubes, one 9-block, number markers 1 to 9

- Ask a child to select two number markers and place them on the dual board below the tens and ones compartments.
- Have another child build the number (54) with 10-blocks and cubes and name it, "54."
- Pick up the 9-block. Say, "54 plus 9 . . . ?" Place the 9-block in the tens compartment.
- Say, "Take a one and add it to the 9 to make 10" (do so).
- The child observes, "Oh! So the tens go up and the ones go down 1 . . . 63!"
- Continue for several cycles.
- Remove the blocks from the dual board.
- Have children take turns building and recording other 2-place numbers in the dual board and adding 9 to them.

LESSON 63. Adding 9 in the Number Track

Purpose: To discover that adding 9 to a number gives a sum that is 1 less than if 10 had been added to that number.
Group Activity
Materials: number track 1 to 50, two sets of number blocks 1 to 10

- Place any number block in the first decade, perhaps 3, and add a 10-block to it.
- Ask, "3 and 10 are . . . ?" A child responds, "13."
- Remove the 10-block.
- Next, add a 9-block to the 3-block.
- Ask, "3 and 9 are . . . ?" The child says, "12; you go down 1."
- Have the children figure out several higher-decade facts by pushing the combination into higher decades by inserting a 10-block in the first section.
- Ask, "13 and 9 are . . . ?" (22). Move up again, "23 and 9 are . . . ?" (32).

Plus 10, Plus 9 (see p. 65)
What Number Did I Hide? (see p. 65)
Adding 9 in the Dual Board (see above)
Workbook Page: A and B. Go over the illustrations. The children finish the page independently.

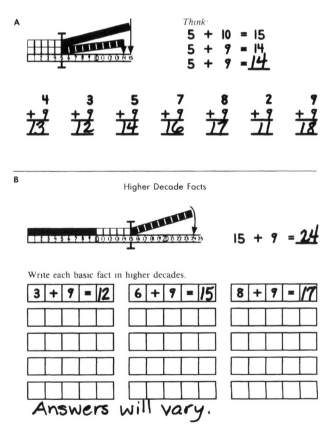

LESSON 64. Adding 8 in the Number Track

Purpose: To discover that adding 8 to a number gives a sum 2 less than if 10 had been added to that number.

Group Activity

Materials: number track 1 to 50, two sets of number blocks 1 to 10
- Add 8 to the even number blocks 8, 6, and 4.
- Elicit that the answer contains the next lower even number.
- Add 8 to the odd number blocks 9, 7, 5, and 3.
- Elicit that the answer contains the next lower odd number because 8 is 2 less than 10.
- To get a higher-decade fact, put a 10-block in the first decade and push the combination up: 3 + 8 = 11, 13 + 8 = 21, ... 33 + 8 = 41.

Stop-and-Go Game

Materials: stop-and-go cube, paper cup
- On the chalkboard write team names and a basic +8 fact:

  Blue Team   Red Team
  5 + 8 = 13   6 + 8 = 14

- The first player to toss the stop-and-go cube from the cup and get Go writes the +8 fact in a higher decade under her team's name.
- Stop means no written turn (but the combination can be given orally).
- The team to write the most facts wins.

Workbook Page: A and B. Go over the illustrations. The children finish the page independently.

ADDING 8 IN THE NUMBER TRACK

A   *Think:*
4 + 10 = 14
4 + 8 = 12
4 + 8 = __12__

8	3	5	7	6	9	4
+8	+8	+8	+8	+8	+8	+8
16	11	13	15	14	17	12

B   Higher Decade Facts

14 + 8 = __22__

Write each basic fact in higher decades.

Answers will vary.

LESSON 65. Subtracting 9 in the Number Track

Purpose: To discover that when 9 is subtracted from any number the answer is 1 more than when 10 is subtracted from that number.

Group Activity

Materials: number track 1 to 20, number blocks 1 to 10
- Place a 3-block and a 10-block in the number track.
- As you subtract the 10-block, say, "13 minus 10 ... ?" (3).
- Now, to the 3-block, add blocks 1 and 9.
- Call on a child to demonstrate 13 minus 9.
- He subtracts the 9-block and says, "13 − 9 = 4."
- Elicit that 4 is 1 more than when you subtract 10 from 13.
- Have the children subtract 9 from other teen numbers.

Solving for X

Materials: same as above plus a paper strip to cover the blocks for 3 + 1. Write X on it.
- Place in the track the blocks for 3 + 1 + 9 and cover 3 + 1 with the strip of paper.
- Write on the board X = 13 − 9; have a child read it and subtract the 9-block; this leaves the strip of paper.
- The child looks under the strip and writes what she sees, X = 4.

Workbook Page: Go over the answers orally. The children finish the page independently.

SUBTRACTING 9 IN THE NUMBER TRACK

A   *Think:*
13 − 10 = 3
13 − 9 = 4
13 − 9 = __4__

15	17	13	11	16	14	18
−9	−9	−9	−9	−9	−9	−9
6	8	4	2	7	5	9

B   Find X.

X = 16 − 9   X = 15 − 10   X = 11 − 9
X = __7__   X = __5__   X = __2__

X = 14 − 9   X = 17 − 10   X = 12 − 9
X = __5__   X = __7__   X = __3__

X = 15 − 9   X = 17 − 9   X = 18 − 9
X = __6__   X = __8__   X = __9__

X = 13 − 9   X = 9 − 9   X = 13 − 10
X = __4__   X = __0__   X = __3__

LESSON 66. Subtracting 8 in the Number Track

SUBTRACTING 8 IN THE NUMBER TRACK

Purpose: To discover that when 8 is subtracted from any number, the answer is 2 more than when 10 is subtracted from that number. To test subtracting 8 or 9 from teen numbers.

Group Activity

Materials: number track 1 to 20, number blocks 1 to 10
- In the track make 15 with a 5-block and a 10-block.
- Ask, "15 minus 10 is . . . ?" and have a child demonstrate it.
- Now, add blocks for 2 + 8 to the 5-block.
- Call on a child to subtract the 8-block from 15.
- Elicit that when you subtract 8 the answer will always be 2 bigger than if you had subtracted 10.
- Have the children subtract 8 from other teen numbers by setting up the experiment in the same way.

Workbook Page: A. Review orally. Have the children tell the number 2 more than the number you say. Say, "5" (7); say, "4" (6); and so on. This helps children with the answer to 15 − 8 = 7 and 14 − 8 = 6.

B. Prepare children for the test by having them circle the examples of subtracting 8. This helps them concentrate on what they are doing. The children finish the test independently.

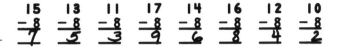

A

Think:
15 − 10 = 5
15 − 8 = 7
15 − 8 = 7

15	13	11	17	14	16	12	10
−8	−8	−8	−8	−8	−8	−8	−8
7	5	3	9	6	8	4	2

B

TEST

15	18	11	17	14	16	13	12
−8	−9	−8	−8	−9	−9	−8	−9
7	9	3	9	5	7	5	3

12	18	17	13	11	16	14	15
−8	−8	−8	−9	−9	−8	−8	−9
4	10	9	4	2	8	6	6

11	11	17	13	17	15	15	13
−9	−8	−8	−8	−9	−8	−9	−9
2	3	9	5	8	7	6	4

LESSON 67. Test

Purpose: To solve problems requiring subtraction for their solution.

Note: Children show they understand how to solve problems when they can make up similar problems.

Group Activity

Materials: 10 index cards (two each of numbers 11 to 15), two sets of number markers 6 to 9, two boxes
- Divide the class into two teams.
- Arrange numerals facedown in two boxes; box A contains teen numbers 11 to 15, box B, two sets of number markers 6 to 9.
- On the chalkboard write the names of two kinds of problems and discuss a problem of each type:

    What Are the Rest?   How Many More Are Needed?

- Pass boxes A and B to the first player.
- The child selects a number from box B, perhaps 9, and a teen number from box A, perhaps 14.
- The child makes up a story using the subtraction fact 14 − 9 and asks either question, How Many More Are Needed? or What Are the Rest? Another child writes the example under the correct heading.
- The problem might be: The pet store had 14 cages. There were 9 empty cages. The rest had animals in them. How many cages had animals in them? (14 − 9 = 5; 5 cages had animals in them).

Workbook Page: Go over the problems if necessary. The children finish the test independently.

TEST

① Dinah has **2** dimes. She wants a sticker that costs **18¢**. How much change will she get back?

20
−18
2

She will get **2**¢ change.

② There were **17** children in the classroom. **8** children went to the playground. How many were left in the classroom?

17
−8
9

There were **9** children left in the room.

③ Shawn has **15** pet mice. **9** mice are white; the rest are gray. How many gray mice does Shawn have?

15
−9
6

Shawn has **6** gray mice.

④ Mom needs **14** stamps for her letters. She has **9** stamps. How many more does she need?

14
−9
5

Mom needs **5** more stamps.

⑤ Kate wants an apple that costs **15¢**. She has only **9¢** in her pocket. How much more money does she need?

15
−9
6

She needs **6**¢ more.

⑥ Lee picked **11** apples. Pat picked **9**. How many more apples did Lee pick?

11
−9
2

Lee picked **2** more apples than Pat.

UNIT 12. SUMS OF 11 AND 12; SUBTRACTING FROM 11 AND 12

Lessons in this unit:
68. Combinations That Make 11
69. Subtracting from 11
70. Combinations That Make 12
71. Subtracting from 12

By Unit 12 children have covered three quarters of the 72 addition and subtraction facts in the teens (see pp. 89 and 90). The addition facts were studied in four separate groups: adding to 9, adding 9 to numbers, adding to 8, and adding 8 to numbers. The subtraction facts were studied in two groups: subtracting 9 from numbers and subtracting 8 from numbers.

The facts in Unit 12 are grouped as follows: facts with sums of 11, subtracting from 11, facts with sums of 12, and subtracting from 12. Although these groups cover thirty facts, the children have already studied half of them. They should feel a sense of mastery when they realize that half the facts they are meeting are familiar ones presented in a new context.

Combinations That Make 11 and 12

In this unit children build the stair from 1 to 10 in the 20-tray and then fill in the stair to form the combinations that make 10. To get the combinations that make 11 they move the upper set of blocks up 1 step. They see that each row is completed by a block 1 bigger than the block required for the combinations that make 10. To form the combinations that make 12, they build the combinations that make 10 and move the upper set of blocks up 2 steps. Thus they discover that if they know the 10-facts, they can easily figure out the 11-facts and the 12-facts.

Subtracting from 11 and 12

When children know the component parts of 11 and 12, they can figure out the corresponding subtraction facts (5 + 6 = 11; 11 − 5 = 6 and 11 − 6 = 5).

Combinations on the Clock Face

On the clock face, the numbers across from each other add up to 12. Children find this very exciting.

Higher-Decade Facts

As with the other teen facts, children transfer these combinations to higher decades.

GAMES AND DEMONSTRATIONS

Moving Up in the 20-Tray (use with Lesson 68)
Materials: 20-tray, two sets of number blocks 1 to 10
- The children build the stair 1 to 10 and fill in the stair with blocks to show the combinations that make 10.
- Next, move each of the top blocks up 1 step, one block at a time.
- Point to the combination 9 + 1; move the 1-cube up 1 step onto the 10-block, thus building 11.
- Move the 2-block up 1, and add it to the 9-block.
- Elicit, "9 and 1 made 10, but 9 and 2 make 11."
- Move each block up 1 to make these combinations: 10 + 1, 9 + 2, 8 + 3, 7 + 4, 6 + 5, . . . 2 + 9.

Combinations That Make 11 (use with Lesson 68)
Materials: 20-tray, two sets of number blocks 1 to 10
- Scatter the blocks on the table.
- In the 20-tray build the stair from 1 to 10.
- Add the 1-block to 10 and elicit, "10 + 1 = 11."
- Add the 2-block to 9 and elicit, "9 + 2 = 11."
* Ask, "8 needs what to make 11?" (3).
- Continue to ask for one combination after another until you have all the combinations that make 11.

LESSON 68. Combinations That Make 11

Purpose: To discover the combinations that make 11.
Group Activity
Moving Up in the 20-Tray (see p. 69)
Combinations That Make 11 (see p. 69)
Hiding Game in the Number Track
Materials: number track 1 to 20, two sets of number blocks 1 to 10
- Hide two blocks that make 11, such as 7 and 4.
- Say, "I have 11 altogether" (point to number 11 on the track).
- Say, "In one hand is 7" (put it in the track).
- Ask, "What does 7 need to make 11?"
- The child reasons that 7 + 3 makes 10, so 7 needs 4 to make 11.
- Ask for all the combinations that make 11 in this way.
- Elicit that 11 is 1 bigger than 10. Therefore, the added block each time must be 1 bigger than if they were making 10.

Workbook Page: A. Go over the illustration and examples.
B. Have some higher-decade facts suggested orally first; then let children think of their own higher-decade facts.

COMBINATIONS THAT MAKE 11

A

Think:
7 + 3 = 10
7 + (3+1) = 11
7 + _4_ = 11

8 + _3_ = 11

9 + _2_ = 11

B
Higher Decade Facts

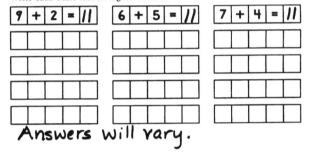

18 + 3 = _21_

Write each basic fact in higher decades.

| 9 + 2 = 11 | 6 + 5 = 11 | 7 + 4 = 11 |

Answers will vary.

LESSON 69. Subtracting from 11

Purpose: To study the facts that result when the numbers 2 to 9 are subtracted from 11.
Group Activity
Analysis of the 11-Facts
Materials: 20-tray, two sets of number blocks 1 to 10
- Build the combinations that make 11 in the 20-tray.
- Move aside the combination 10 + 1; say, "This is 11."
- Move aside 2 + 9 and 9 + 2 (already studied).
- Move aside 3 + 8 and 8 + 3 (already studied).
- Move aside 4 + 7 and 7 + 4; these are new facts.
- Point to the pair of facts in the center: 5 + 6 and 6 + 5. Elicit that in the center of every *odd* number is a pair of neighbors.

Scarf Game in the Number Track
Materials: number track 1 to 20, number blocks 1 to 10, scarf
- When the children's eyes are closed, place two blocks in the number track, perhaps 5 and 6, and cover them with a scarf.
- Say, "Open your eyes. The blocks I hid make 11. If I take 6 away (do so), what is left?" (5).
- A child states, "11 minus 6 is 5," and lifts the scarf.
- Have children take the role of teacher in this game.

Workbook Page: A and **B.** Children work on sections A and B independently.
C. Review problems of Finding the Rest (see lesson 20). The children finish the problems independently.

SUBTRACTING FROM 11

A
 11 − 4 = _7_

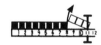 11 − 3 = _8_

 11 − 2 = _9_

B
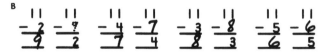

C
Lynn has 11 hamsters. 5 are brown; the rest are spotted.
How many are spotted?

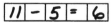

Lynn has **6** spotted hamsters.

11 children are coming to the party.
Peter has only 3 paper plates.
How many plates will he have to buy?

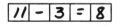

Peter will have to buy **8** paper plates.

LESSON 70. Combinations That Make 12

Purpose: To discover the combinations that make 12.
Group Activity
Materials: 20-tray, two sets of number blocks 1 to 10
- Build the stair from 1 to 10 in the 20-tray.
- Point to the 10-block; add a 2-block to make 12.
- Point to the 9-block; ask, "What does 9 need to make 12?"
- A child adds the 3-block and states, "9 + 3 = 12."
- Continue until all the facts have been demonstrated.

Hiding Game in the Number Track
Materials: number track 1 to 20, number blocks 1 to 10
- Hide two blocks that make 12, such as 7 and 5.
- Place the 7-block in the number track.
- Ask, "What will 7 need to make 12?"
- The child reasons that 7 + 3 makes 10, but 7 will need 3 and 2 more to reach 12, and answers, "7 + 5 = 12."
- Continue with other pairs of blocks that make 12.
- Draw a blank clock face on the chalkboard.
- Write each number as you name it: First, the number on the left, then the number on the opposite side. Say, "11 and 1, 10 and 2, 9 and 3, 8 and 4, 7 and 5, 6 and 6—each pair makes 12!"

Workbook Page: Go over the page first. The children finish the page independently.

COMBINATIONS THAT MAKE 12

A

Think:
7 + 3 = 10
7 + (3+2) = 12
7 + _5_ = 12
8 + _4_ = 12

B Look at the clock! The numbers across from each other add up to **12**.

9 + _3_ = 12   3 + _9_ = 12
8 + _4_ = 12   4 + _8_ = 12
7 + _5_ = 12   5 + _7_ = 12
6 + _6_ = 12

C Higher Decade Facts

   18 + 4 = _22_

Write each basic fact in a higher decade.

| 6 + 6 = 12 | 7 + 5 = 12 | 8 + 4 = 12 |

Answers will vary.

LESSON 71. Subtracting from 12

Purpose: To study the facts that result when the numbers 3 to 9 are subtracted from 12.
Group Activity
Analysis of the 12-Facts
Materials: 20-tray, two sets of number blocks 1 to 10
- Build the combinations that make 12 in the 20-tray.
- Move aside 10 + 2 and say, "This is 12."
- Move aside 3 + 9 and 9 + 3 (already studied).
- Move aside 4 + 8 and 8 + 4 (already studied).
- Point out that 5 + 7 and 7 + 5 are new facts.
- Elicit that in the middle of every even number is a double, "6 and 6 make 12."

Scarf Game in the Number Track
Materials: number track 1 to 20, number blocks 1 to 10, scarf
- When the children's eyes are closed, place two blocks in the number track, perhaps 7 and 5, and cover them with a scarf.
- Say, "Open your eyes. The blocks I hid make 12. If I take 5 away, (do so) what is left?" (7).
- A child states, "12 minus 5 leaves 7," and lifts the scarf.
- Children like to take the role of teacher in this game.

Workbook Page: **A** and **B**. Go over these examples first.
C. Review the problems on Finding the Rest (see Lesson 20). You subtract one part in order to find the other part.
The children finish the page independently.

SUBTRACTING FROM 12

A
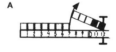   12 − 5 = _7_
                         12 − _7_ = 5

   12 − 4 = _8_
                         12 − _8_ = 4

   12 − 3 = _9_
                         12 − _9_ = 3

B
12	12	12	12	12	12	12
−6	−5	−7	−4	−8	−3	−9
6	7	5	8	4	9	3

C The cook needs a dozen eggs. He has **6** eggs. How many eggs will he buy?

| 12 − 6 = 6 |

He will buy _6_ eggs.

Teresa asked **12** children to her party. **4** children could not come. How many children came to her party?

| 12 − 4 = 8 |

_8_ children came to Teresa's party.

UNIT 13. MORE TEEN FACTS

Lessons in this unit:
72. Adding Doubles
73. Adding Neighbors
74. Subtracting from the Sums of Doubles and Neighbors
75. Remainder of 9; Remainder of 8
76. Column Addition
77. Test: Addition Facts
78. Test: Subtraction Facts
79. Test: Subtraction Facts

Doubles and Neighbors

This final group of related facts reviews some combinations covered in previous groups: adding to 9, adding to 8, and combinations that make 11 and 12. The new facts are $7 + 7 = 14$, $6 + 7 = 13$, $7 + 6 = 13$, and the related subtraction facts.

Doubles

Each even number in the teens has a double in the middle: $6 + 6$, $7 + 7$, $8 + 8$, $9 + 9$, and $10 + 10$. The doubles are pivotal facts that enable children to figure out the more difficult facts called "neighbors."

Neighbors

Each odd number in the teens has two combinations in the middle. For example, in the combinations that make 11 there are two facts in the middle, $5 + 6$ and $6 + 5$. 5 and 6 are neighbors. The sum of consecutive numbers is an odd number.

Relating Neighbors to Doubles

In this unit children study the relationship between a double and the neighbor on either side. For instance, if $6 + 7 = 13$ has been forgotten, the child can reason that if $6 + 6 = 12$, then $6 + 7$ must be 13.

GAMES AND DEMONSTRATIONS

Setting Up the Sticker Sandwich Game (use after Lesson 73)
How to Make a Doubles and Neighbors Board:
On cardboard, trace pairs of blocks; begin with $5 + 6$, then double 6, $6 + 7$, double 7, and so forth (see illustration).

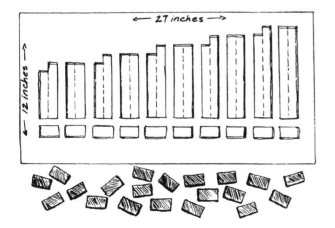

Materials: doubles and neighbors board, a 5-block, four each of blocks 6, 7, 8, and 9, three 10-blocks, five dominoes labeled 12, 14, 16, 18, and 20 (sums of doubles), five dominoes labeled 11, 13, 15, 17, and 19 (sums of neighbors), ten dominoes labeled with equations $5 + 6 =$, $6 + 6 =$, ... $10 + 10 =$ (one for each pair of blocks in the doubles and neighbors board)

- Scatter the blocks and even numbered dominoes (facedown) on the table.
- A child selects a domino (12), puts it in the board with the corresponding pair of blocks, and says, "$6 + 6 = 12$."
- Children complete all the combinations of blocks for the doubles first (12, 14, 16, 18, 20).
- Scatter the odd numbered dominoes (facedown) on the table.
- A child selects a domino (17), puts it in the board with the corresponding pair of blocks, and says, "$8 + 9 = 17$."
- When all the blocks for teen numbers and all the dominoes with sums are in place, scatter the ten equation dominoes (facedown) on the table.
- A child selects a domino ($7 + 8 =$), puts it below the sum domino, and puts a sticker between the blocks for 7 and 8.
- Continue until there is a sticker between every two blocks.

Note: Now you are ready to play the Sticker Sandwich Game.

GAMES AND DEMONSTRATIONS

Sticker Sandwich Game (use after Lesson 73)
Note: Follow the preparation for this game on the previous page. You have dominoes for ten sums and ten equations. Elicit that each odd number can have two combinations (5 + 6 = 11 and 6 + 5 = 11), but explain that the game uses only one combination for each pair of blocks.
- Remove all twenty dominoes and turn them facedown.
- Players take turns selecting dominoes and placing them below the proper pairs of blocks.
* Call on a child; say, "Pick a domino! What did you get?"
- The child says, "7 plus 8 is 15! I get a sticker sandwich!" (because 15 is already there. Getting two matching dominoes allows the player to remove the sticker from between, for example, blocks 7 and 8 and make a sticker sandwich by putting the sticker between the two dominoes labeled 15 and 7 + 8 =.)
- At the end of the game, children may keep their stickers.

Note: Use the same kind of sticker for every player. This is a popular game!

Snake Game—Remainder of 9 (use with Lesson 75)
Materials: number track 1 to 20, number blocks 1 to 10, ten cubes, an extra 9-block, nine cards labeled 11 to 19
- Divide the group into two teams.
- Turn the cards facedown.
- Place blocks for 9 + 1 in the track.
- A child selects and reads a number, perhaps 15.
- To make 15, he adds a 5-block to blocks 9 + 1.
* Say, "You want 9 left. What can you take from 15 to leave 9?"
- The child subtracts the 5-block plus 1 more, and says, "15 minus 6 leaves 9."
- These blocks, 5 and 1, are then added to his team's snake of blocks.
- Other children take turns demonstrating a similar subtraction example and adding blocks to their snake.
- Write the following examples on the chalkboard:

11	19	17	18	16	14	12	13	15
9	9	9	9	9	9	9	9	9

- Children take turns writing the amount subtracted in each example.

LESSON 72. Adding Doubles

Purpose: To study the facts that result when the numbers 6 to 10 are added to themselves.

Group Activity

Materials: doubles and neighbors board, two each of blocks 6 to 10

- Give each child two blocks the same size.
- Ask, "Who has the blocks that fit here?" (point to the space for double 6).
- A child puts the blocks in place and says, "6 and 6."
- When all the doubles are lying on the board, leave them in place for the next activity.

Doubles in the Number Track

Materials: number track 1 to 20, dominoes labeled 12, 14, 16, 18, and 20 (sums of doubles), doubles and neighbors board filled with blocks for the doubles, equation dominoes

- Measure the first double, 6 + 6, in the track.
- A child says, "12," selects the domino for 12, and puts it and the blocks back in the board.
- Children do the same for each double.
- Scatter the equation dominoes on the table.
- Children match each equation domino with the correct blocks and the domino with their sum (12 goes with 6 + 6 =).

Workbook Page: Go over the page. The children finish the page independently.

ADDING DOUBLES

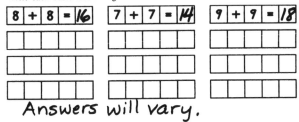

LESSON 73. Adding Neighbors

Purpose: To discover the two consecutive numbers (neighbors) that make up each odd number: 11, 13, 15, 17, and 19.

Group Activity

Materials: doubles and neighbors board, one 5-block, one 10-block, two each of blocks 6 to 9, dominoes labeled 11, 13, 15, 17, 19 (sums of neighbors), equation dominoes

- Build a stair of blocks from 5 to 10. Say, "5 and 6 are neighbors; they live next to each other in the stair."
- Give each child two neighbors (5 and 6, 6 and 7, 7 and 8, 8 and 9, 9 and 10).
- Ask, "Who has neighbors that fit here?" (point to 11).
- A child puts the blocks in place and says, "5 and 6."
- Ask for other neighbors: 6 + 7, 7 + 8, 8 + 9, 9 + 10.
- Scatter the dominoes with sums.
- Since the doubles are known, the children reason that since 6 and 6 are 12, 6 and 7 make 13.
- They put in place all the dominoes with sums.
- Scatter the equation dominoes, and have children match them to blocks.
- Elicit the reverse fact for each pair of blocks: 6 + 7 = 13 and 7 + 6 = 13, etc.

Sticker Sandwich Game (see pp. 72 and 73).

Workbook Page: Go over the page. The children finish the page independently.

ADDING NEIGHBORS

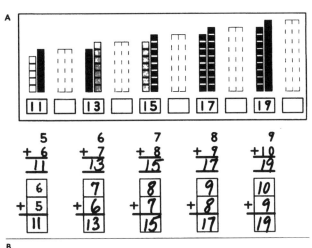

LESSON 74. Subtracting from the Sums of Doubles and Neighbors

Purpose: To discover the subtraction facts that result when one of two parts is subtracted from a double or from two consecutive numbers (neighbors) in the teens.

Group Activity
Hiding Game (to check addition facts)
Materials: doubles and neighbors board, a 5-block, four each of blocks 6, 7, 8, and 9, three 10-blocks, five dominoes with sums of neighbors

- Hide two consecutive blocks such as 8 and 9.
- Call on a child. Say, "I have 17 altogether. In one hand is 8; what is in the other hand?" (9).
- The child places the blocks in the board.

Scarf Game (to check subtraction facts)
Materials: doubles and neighbors board filled with blocks for the odd numbers and dominoes with their sums (11, 13, 15, 17, 19), scarf

- Cover a pair of blocks with a scarf.
- Say, "I am hiding 15. If I take 7 away (do so), what is left?" (8). Remove the scarf for checking.
- Elicit that you can also ask, "15 − 8 = __?" (7).

Workbook Page: Go over **B**. Elicit that you have two combinations for neighbors because you can subtract either block. The children finish the page independently.

SUBTRACTING FROM THE SUMS OF DOUBLES AND NEIGHBORS

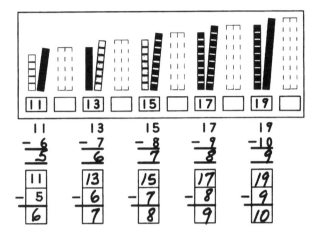

LESSON 75. Remainder of 9; Remainder of 8

Purpose: To discover that when working with teen numbers to get a remainder of 9, you must subtract a number 1 greater than the digit in the ones place. To get a remainder of 8 you must subtract a number 2 greater than the digit in the ones place.

Group Activity
Materials: number track 1 to 20, number blocks 1 to 10, ten cubes, an extra 8-block and 9-block

- Place blocks 10 + 3 in the track; demonstrate 13 − 3 = 10.
- Replace the 10-block with the blocks for 9 + 1.
- Ask, "If you want to have 9 left, what must you subtract from 13?"
- The child sees you must subtract 3 + 1 (13 − 4 = 9).

Snake Game—Remainder of 9 (see p. 73)
Remainder of 8
Materials: number track 1 to 20, number blocks 1 to 10

- In the number track build the teen number 13 with 8 + 2 and 3.
- Ask, "If you want 8 left, what will you take from 13?"
- A child sees that you must subtract 3 + 2, or 5, and states, "13 − 5 leaves 8."

Workbook Page: Elicit that these combinations have been studied in two other groups: neighbors and combinations that make 11 and 12.

The children finish the page independently.

REMAINDER OF 9; REMAINDER OF 8

A Remainder of 9

Think
13 − 3 = 10
13 − 4 = 9

15	11	13	14	17	17
−6	−2	−3	−5	−7	−8
9	9	10	9	10	9

18	16	12	12	13	19
−9	−7	−3	−2	−4	−9
9	9	9	10	9	10

B Remainder of 8

Think
13 − 3 = 10
13 − (3+2) = 8
13 −  = 8

13	15	12	11	17	14
−5	−7	−4	−3	−9	−6
8	8	8	8	8	8

75

LESSON 76. Column Addition

Purpose: To discover how to solve addition examples with more than two addends.

Group Activity
Materials: number track 1 to 40, two sets of number blocks 1 to 10
- Write on the chalkboard: 4 + 5 + 3 + 4 = ___.
- Have a child line up these blocks along the track.
- Explain that as you insert block after block into the track, a child will announce the partial sum each time.
- Insert blocks for 4 + 5 (9); add 3 (12); add 4 (16). Write the sum on the chalkboard.

Exit Game
Materials: number track 1 to 40, four colored cubes for each player to use as "cars," two cubes with numbers 0 to 5 and 5 to 10 printed on their faces
- If players land on 10, 20, or 30 (exits), they go back to 0.
- Each move is determined by tossing the two numbered cubes.
- If a player rolls 5 and 7, she may put a "car" on 5 and another on 7, or just one on 12. Or one "car" may be moved up 5 and another up 7, or one moved up 12 units. Do not allow children to count out their moves by ones.
- The winner is the first to get all 4 "cars" to 40. Players must throw the exact number needed to reach 40.
- A player who lands on another "car" rides piggyback until the next turn.

Workbook Page: The children finish the page independently.

COLUMN ADDITION

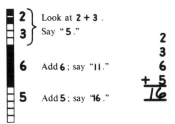

A A fast way to add:
Do not say,
"2 + 3 = 5."

Look at 2 + 3. Say "5."
Add 6; say "11."
Add 5; say "16."

```
  2
  3
  6
 +5
 ――
 16
```

B

```
  8    9    6    9    7    6    8    1
  8    9    6    9    3    4    2    9
  6    8    9    0    4    3    2    3
 +8   +4   +7   +4   +4   +6   +3   +4
 ――   ――   ――   ――   ――   ――   ――   ――
 30   30   28   22   18   19   15   17
```

```
  7    8    8    4    8    5    9    8
  5    4    3    8    6    8    8    0
  9    6    5    9    7    9    3    3
 +8   +4   +6   +9   +8   +8   +9   +9
 ――   ――   ――   ――   ――   ――   ――   ――
 29   22   22   30   29   30   29   20
```

C In a game of darts, Julia scored 6, 7, 5, and 8. Jacob scored 5, 9, 7, and 3. Who won the game?

Julia
```
  6
  7
  5
 +8
 ――
 26
```

Jacob
```
  5
  9
  7
 +3
 ――
 24
```

The winner was __Julia__.

LESSON 77. Test: Addition Facts

Purpose: To test mastery of 56 of the basic 100 addition facts.

Group Activity
Facts with Sums of 10 or Less
Materials: 10-box, number blocks
- Review facts with a sum of 10 and their reverse facts in the 10-box.
- Review facts with sums of 9, 8, 7, and 5 with the number blocks.
- Review facts with sums of consecutive numbers (2 + 3) and their reverse facts (see p. 11).

Teen Facts
Materials: 20-tray, eleven 10-blocks, two sets of number blocks 1 to 9

Note: All 36 teen facts are tested.
- Build the combinations that make 10 in the 20-tray, then move the top set of blocks up 1 step (facts with a sum of 11, see p. 69).
- Move the top set of blocks up 1 again (facts with a sum of 12, see p. 71).
- Continue moving the upper set of blocks up 1.
- Children recite the facts with sums of 13, 14, 15, 16, 17, and 18.
- Elicit that the number of facts to learn decreases each time.

Workbook Page: Go over the examples orally. The children finish the page independently.

TEST: ADDITION FACTS

```
 9    8    4    7    6    5    9    6
+9   +3   +7   +6   +8   +6   +3   +9
――   ――   ――   ――   ――   ――   ――   ――
18   11   11   13   14   11   12   15

 4    3    8    6    2    7    8    3
+5   +4   +5   +3   +7   +9   +6   +5
――   ――   ――   ――   ――   ――   ――   ――
 9    7   13    9    9   16   14    8

 8    9    5    7    9    3    4    7
+0   +4   +8   +2   +0   +8   +6   +5
――   ――   ――   ――   ――   ――   ――   ――
 8   13   13    9    9   11   10   12

 2    8    6    2    7    9    5    8
+6   +7   +6   +8   +3   +7   +2   +8
――   ――   ――   ――   ――   ――   ――   ――
 8   15   12   10   10   16    7   16

 2    4    3    9    7    5    2    6
+9   +9   +6   +6   +8   +3   +5   +7
――   ――   ――   ――   ――   ――   ――   ――
11   13    9   15   15    8    7   13

 7    9    6    8    5    2    3    6
+7   +2   +4   +9   +7   +3   +7   +5
――   ――   ――   ――   ――   ――   ――   ――
14   11   10   17   12    5   10   11

 3    4    7    9    9    7    8    5
+9   +8   +4   +5   +8   +3   +4   +9
――   ――   ――   ――   ――   ――   ――   ――
12   12   11   14   17   10   12   14
```

LESSON 78. Test: Subtraction Facts

Purpose: To test mastery of 32 of the basic subtraction facts.

Group Activity

Subtracting from 10 or Less
Review subtraction facts (see pp. 8 to 10).

Teen Facts
- Here is an unforgettable demonstration of a difficult fact, 13 − 5 = 8. Say, "8." (Hold up 8 fingers—your left hand plus 3 fingers of your right.)
- Say, "Plus 5." A child facing you extends 5 fingers of the right hand opposite your left hand.
- Continue, "The sum is . . . ?" Clasp together the two opposite hands. 10 clasped fingers and 3 on your right hand give 13.
- Now say, "13 minus 5 is . . . ?" The child removes a hand of 5 fingers.
- Say, "8 fingers remain: 13 − 5 = 8."
- Demonstrate 13 − 8 = 5.

Scarf Game

Materials: two sets of number blocks 1 to 10, scarf
- Under a scarf hide all the combinations that make a teen number, perhaps 11.
- Children take turns asking for two blocks that make 11 ("Give me 5 and 6").
- Place each combination on the table where it will lie as you build all the combinations that make 11. (Place 5 + 6 in the middle; this framework indicates which combinations are still missing.)

Workbook Page: Go over the examples orally. The children finish the page independently.

LESSON 79. Test: Subtraction Facts

Purpose: To test mastery of an additional 32 basic subtraction facts.

Group Activity

Subtracting from 10 (Set A)

Materials: pattern boards 7 and 6, twenty cubes

Note: The following demonstration clears up two combinations that children often confuse: 10 − 3 and 10 − 4.
- Fill each pattern with cubes so there are 10.
- Children see that removing the odd number 3 leaves the odd number 7, while subtracting the even number 4 leaves the even number 6.

Teen Numbers
- Review subtracting from teen numbers by playing a hiding game such as the one in Lesson 78.
- Ask the children to write as many facts as they can from a certain group of related facts, perhaps with a remainder of 9. Elicit that the number subtracted is always 1 bigger than the ones digit of the teen number (see Lesson 75).
- Give each child a different teen number; have them write as many subtraction examples as possible.

Workbook Page: Go over the examples orally. The children finish the page independently.

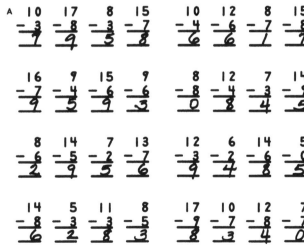

77

UNIT 14. REGROUPING IN ADDITION AND SUBTRACTION

Lessons in this unit:
80. Regrouping in Addition
81. Regrouping in Addition
82. Regrouping in Addition
83. Regrouping in Column Addition
84. Regrouping in Subtraction
85. Regrouping in Subtraction
86. Regrouping in Subtraction
87. Test

Addition: Carrying Over

Unit 15 deals with procedures more familiarly known to the previous generation as "carrying" and "borrowing." Today these names have been replaced by the word *regrouping*. In our system of positional notation, when the amount in one column exceeds base 10, it can only be expressed in two denominations (that is, by a 2-place number); the amount is regrouped. This procedure occurs between any two denominations, tens and ones, hundreds and tens, thousands and hundreds, and so forth.

Thus, when dealing with a total in the ones column, such as twelve ones, we exchange ten of the ones for 1 ten and carry it to the tens column where we add it to the tens already there. When the word *regrouping* is used, we say, "12 is regrouped as 1 ten and 2 ones." Many teachers extend this by saying, "Carry 1 ten to the tens column." The term *carry* seems to explain the procedure in a more satisfying way to students since it describes the action that results from adding two numbers.

In subtraction, the procedure is reversed. Many people still use the old term *borrowing*. We will use "carry back 1 ten" since it corresponds more accurately to what the children will be doing with the materials. It also describes what happens in regrouping: we take 1 ten from the tens and regroup it by carrying it back and writing it in the ones column.

Since the materials enable the children to act out these words with the materials when they are learning them, the terms make sense. *Carrying back* makes it clear that the procedure has the exact opposite effect to the term *carrying over* in addition. It is just this contrast between carrying in addition and carrying back, or borrowing, in subtraction that is not brought out when the term *regrouping* is used for both procedures.

Children with learning differences, and there are many, may find exchanging 10 single ones for 1 solid ten impossible to understand; they see they are equal in length only—they do not think they should be equally exchangeable. In such cases it is worth the trouble to fashion a hollow shield out of blue paper, fit it exactly over the 10 cubes and carry this mock 10-block to the tens compartment. The children can then accept that this mock ten can be exchanged for a solid 10-block.

The dual board thus becomes the framework through which the experiences of the past and those of the future are linked. At first the children built only 2-place numbers in the dual board, with tens and cubes. Now they will learn new procedures: in addition, when to regroup too many ones into tens and ones; in subtraction, how to regroup a ten as ones when they need more ones to subtract from.

Regrouping When the Key Number Is Not Ten

The experiments in this unit leave the children with clear basic concepts that they can use not only when ten is the base, or key amount, but with other key amounts. Here are some examples which often confuse children:

```
  2 lbs. 4 oz.      3 ft. 6 in.
−       5 oz.    −       9 in.
```

Children who have not fully understood the concept behind regrouping two denominations by carrying back the bigger one, end up with 14 ounces when they carry over 1 from the 2 pounds. It is important to show them that they are exchanging 1 pound for 16 ounces, which they then carry over and add to the 4 ounces already there, giving them 20 ounces to subtract from.

Carrying back 1 foot means exchanging it for 12 inches. Thus, giving the children a clear explanation in the beginning lays a good foundation for their understanding of problems that deal with weights and measures.

GAMES AND DEMONSTRATIONS

Place Value and Carrying in the Dual Board (use before Lesson 80)

Note: In the following demonstration the children learn more about place value by adding cubes in the dual board. They discover that by adding 1 cube after another, they are forced at a certain point to regroup the cubes into 1 ten. The children record the addition of each cube on paper ruled in two columns to correspond to the two compartments of the dual board, tens and ones (units). They know that a numeral or digit written in the left column means tens; in the right column, ones. Thus, the place a digit occupies in a 2-place number (left or right) tells the value of the digit (tens or ones).

Materials: dual board, 10-blocks, cubes, number markers 1 to 9 and 0, paper divided into two columns labeled *tens* and *ones* for each child

- Place 1 cube in the ones compartment of the dual board. The children write 1 in the ones column of their papers.
- Continue to add 1 cube at a time as children write each successive number below the prevous number.
- With the tenth cube, they discover that the ones compartment has a special feature; it holds ten ones, but it is numbered from 1 to 9. They see that the tenth space is different. It is marked with an arrow that means, "Stop! No more than 9 ones can be recorded in the ones column!"
- Ask, "Is there a number marker with a 1-digit number that you can use to record this amount one greater than 9?" (They should realize that there is no such 1-place number.)
- Explain how they must exchange 10 cubes for 1 solid ten and carry the 1 ten to the tens compartment.
- Children record the ten, putting 1 in the tens place and 0 under the now empty ones column (10). They realize that on paper, too, 1 is written in the tens place and 0 in the ones place. Thus, the familiar symbol 10 takes on a deeper meaning.

Your Answer Is Your Score (use with Lesson 85)

Materials: dual board, number markers, two boxes

- Put markers 2 to 9 in a box for the tens digit; put markers 0 to 5 in a box for the ones digit.
- Call on a child. Say, "Pick a number from the tens box (2) and pick a number from the ones box" (3).
- Say, "Now build 23 with tens and ones."
- The child does so.
- Ask, "How much must you subtract from 23 so you will need to regroup?"
- Child, "Well, if I want to subtract 4 ones, I'll have to exchange 1 ten for 10 ones."
- Child does so and now has 13 cubes.
- The child takes 4 cubes away and says, "13 − 4 leaves 9. I have 1 ten and 9 ones. My answer is 19."
- He writes 19 as the score for his team.

LESSON 80. Regrouping in Addition

Purpose: To discover that when there are 10 ones in the ones column of an addition example, you must regroup them.

Group Activity

Materials: dual board, 10-blocks, cubes, number blocks, two sets of number markers 1 to 9 and 0

- Ask a child to build a number such as 39.
- The child puts 3 tens and 9 cubes (or a 9-block) in the dual board and records it with numbers for 39.
- Ask the child to add 1 cube to the 9 cubes of 39.
- Say, "Now there are 10 ones and no 1-digit number to record them with. You must regroup them."
- Exchange the 10 cubes (or blocks 9 + 1) for 1 ten.
- The child carries 1 ten to the tens compartment, records the empty column with 0, and puts number marker 4 in the tens place.
- Show how this is done at the chalkboard, writing the carried 1 ten as a small 1 in the tens column.

Workbook Page: Go over the illustration carefully as it pictures the experiment children have just done with the materials. They write the examples first on paper with half-inch squares as guidelines. Then the children finish the page independently.

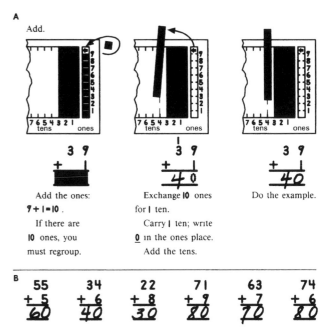

LESSON 81. Regrouping in Addition

Purpose: To discover that when there are more than 10 ones in the ones column of an addition example, you must regroup them.

Materials: dual board, 10-blocks, cubes, number blocks, two sets of number markers 1 to 9 and 0

- Ask a child to build a number such as 36.
- She puts 3 tens and 6 cubes (or the 6-block) in the dual board and records it with numbers for 36.
- Say, "Add 6 to 36." She adds the 6-block or 6 cubes.
- Elicit that there are more than 10 ones (6 + 6 = 12).
- Exchange 10 cubes for 1 ten (or 6 + 6 for 1 ten, 2 ones).
- She carries 1 ten to the tens compartment, puts down 2 cubes in ones place, and records it with 2.
- She then adds the tens and records them with 4.
- The numerals 42 stand below 4 tens, 2 ones.
- Add the example at the chalkboard. Say, "6 and 6 are 12; put down 2, carry 1 ten." Write a small 1 above the 3.
- Compute the total; write 2 in the ones place and 4 in the tens place.

Workbook Page: Go over the illustration step by step first. Write the examples on paper with half-inch squares if the children need extra space and guides for aligning the numbers. Later, the children finish the page independently.

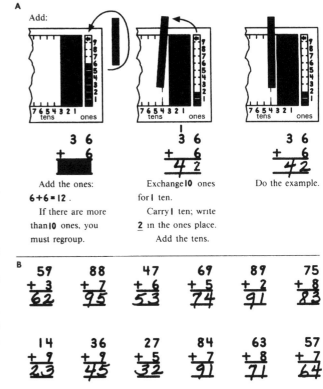

LESSON 82. Regrouping in Addition

Purpose: To add two 2-place numbers in which regrouping takes place.
Group Activity
Materials: dual board, 10-blocks, cubes, number blocks, two sets of number markers 1 to 9, two boxes, labeled Tens Box and Ones Box

- Put number markers 1 to 5 in the tens box and number markers 6 to 9 in the ones box.
- Select two teams. A pair of players from Team A chooses symbols from the boxes; each makes a 2-place number, perhaps 19 and 48, and builds it with blocks.
- As they add the blocks, they carry 1 ten and get 6 tens, 7 ones.
- They write their example on the chalkboard, add ones to ones, and say, "9 + 8 = 17, put down 7, carry 1 ten." Then they add the tens, "1 + 4 + 1 is 6 tens."
- The answer is 67. This is their team's score.
- Team B also chooses symbols and adds two 2-place numbers and records their score.
- Compare the two scores and give a star to the team with the larger sum.
- The team with the most stars wins.

Workbook Page: Go over the illustration. The children finish the page independently.

REGROUPING IN ADDITION

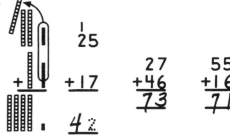

A Add the ones.
Carry 1 ten.
Add the tens.

$$\begin{array}{r}1\\25\\+17\\\hline 42\end{array} \quad \begin{array}{r}27\\+46\\\hline 73\end{array} \quad \begin{array}{r}55\\+16\\\hline 71\end{array}$$

B
$$\begin{array}{r}19\\+48\\\hline 67\end{array} \quad \begin{array}{r}65\\+25\\\hline 90\end{array} \quad \begin{array}{r}58\\+37\\\hline 95\end{array} \quad \begin{array}{r}36\\+29\\\hline 65\end{array} \quad \begin{array}{r}43\\+39\\\hline 82\end{array} \quad \begin{array}{r}25\\+58\\\hline 83\end{array}$$

$$\begin{array}{r}57\\+17\\\hline 74\end{array} \quad \begin{array}{r}28\\+55\\\hline 83\end{array} \quad \begin{array}{r}63\\+18\\\hline 81\end{array} \quad \begin{array}{r}16\\+78\\\hline 94\end{array} \quad \begin{array}{r}18\\+74\\\hline 92\end{array} \quad \begin{array}{r}57\\+35\\\hline 92\end{array}$$

C On Monday 15 children work in the classroom and 17 children have art. How many children are there in all?

$$\begin{array}{r}15\\+17\\\hline 32\end{array}$$

32 children

19 children have red baseball caps. 16 children have blue baseball caps. How many children have baseball caps?

$$\begin{array}{r}19\\+16\\\hline 35\end{array}$$

35 children

LESSON 83. Regrouping in Column Addition

Purpose: To learn to regroup and carry 1 ten in column addition examples with 2-place numbers.
Group Activity
Materials: dual board, 10-blocks, cubes, number blocks, number markers 1 to 9 and 0

- Write on the chalkboard:
  $$\begin{array}{r}34\\14\\+24\end{array}$$
- The children construct each addend with blocks outside the dual board (see workbook for example).
- They add the ones first: 4 + 4 = 8; 8 + 4 = 12.
- The sum is placed in the dual board: 2 ones are put in the ones compartment and 1 ten is carried to the tens compartment.
- The tens are then added—1 carried 10 plus 3 tens (4 tens) + 1 ten (5 tens) + 2 tens (7 tens).
- The dual board now contains 7 tens, 2 ones (72).
- Explain that the written work is done in the same way.
- Students add the numbers on the chalkboard and get the same answer.

Workbook Page: Children should add examples on paper with half-inch squares first. Then they finish the page independently.

REGROUPING IN COLUMN ADDITION

A Add the ones.
Carry 1 ten.
Add the tens.

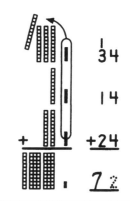

$$\begin{array}{r}1\\34\\14\\+24\\\hline 72\end{array}$$

B
$$\begin{array}{r}12\\25\\+34\\\hline 71\end{array} \quad \begin{array}{r}23\\15\\+35\\\hline 73\end{array} \quad \begin{array}{r}15\\47\\+34\\\hline 96\end{array} \quad \begin{array}{r}16\\20\\+8\\\hline 44\end{array} \quad \begin{array}{r}38\\23\\+28\\\hline 89\end{array} \quad \begin{array}{r}37\\33\\+28\\\hline 98\end{array}$$

C 18 children are in grade 1 at the King School. 33 children are in grade 2, and 36 children are in grade 3. How many children go to the King School?

$$\begin{array}{r}18\\33\\+36\\\hline 87\end{array}$$

87 children

45 girls, 34 boys, and 11 teachers marched in the parade. How many people marched in the parade?

$$\begin{array}{r}45\\34\\+11\\\hline 90\end{array}$$

90 people were in the parade.

LESSON 84. Regrouping in Subtraction

Purpose: To discover that when there are no ones in the ones column of a subtraction example, you must regroup in order to subtract ones from ones.

Group Activity

Materials: dual board, 10-blocks, cubes, number blocks, two sets of number markers 1 to 9 and 0

- Ask a child to build 30 in the dual board.
- The child puts 3 tens in the tens compartment and records it with the markers for 3 and 0.
- Write the example on the chalkboard:

  30
  − 6

- Elicit that they are to take 6 cubes away, but that there are no ones in the ones compartment, so they can't do it.
- Say, "You must regroup. Carry back 1 ten to the tens compartment and exchange it for 10 cubes."
- On the chalkboard, cross out 3, write a small 2 above it, and show the carried 1 by writing 1 next to the 0.
- The child subtracts 6 cubes, which leaves 4 cubes.
- The final amount left is 2 tens, 4 ones (24).
- Carry out the same computation at the board.

Workbook Page: The children write the examples on paper with half-inch squares. Then they finish the page independently.

REGROUPING IN SUBTRACTION

A Subtract.

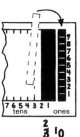

30	²3¹0	30
− 6	− 6	− 6
	24	24

Look at the ones. You cannot take 6 away from 0. You must regroup.

Carry back 1 ten to the ones column. Exchange 1 ten for 10 ones. Write a small 1 next to the 0. Cross out the 3. Write a 2 above the 3. Subtract.

Do the example.

B
70	90	60	20	80	50
−3	−5	−6	−9	−4	−3
67	85	54	11	76	47

50	20	40	90	30	70
−7	−8	−1	−2	−7	−6
43	12	39	88	23	64

LESSON 85. Regrouping in Subtraction

Purpose: To discover that when there are not sufficient ones in the ones column to subtract, you must regroup and carry back 1 ten.

Group Activity

Materials: dual board, 10-blocks, cubes, number blocks, two sets of number markers 1 to 9 and 0

- Ask a child to build 42 with the blocks.
- The child puts 4 tens and 2 ones in the dual board.
- Write the example on the chalkboard:

  42
  − 6

- Elicit that you cannot subtract 6 ones from 2 ones.
- Ask what they could do (carry back 1 ten from the tens column and exchange it for 10 ones).
- The child adds the 10 cubes to the 2 in the ones compartment, making 12 cubes in all.
- Then say, "12 − 6 = 6" (subtract 6 ones; leave 6 ones).
- The remainder is left in the dual board: 3 tens, 6 ones.
- Have a child compute the same example on the chalkboard, crossing out the 3 tens and writing 2 above it.

Your Answer Is Your Score (see p. 79)

Workbook Page: Go over the illustrations. Have the children work on paper with half-inch squares first. They finish the page at a later time.

REGROUPING IN SUBTRACTION

A Subtract.

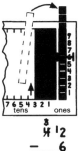

42	³4¹2	42
− 6	− 6	− 6
	36	36

Look at the ones. You cannot take 6 ones away from 2 ones. You must regroup.

Carry back 1 ten to the ones column. Exchange 1 ten for 10 ones. Write a small 1 next to the 2. Cross out the 4. Write a 3 above the 4. Subtract.

Do the example.

B
28	45	64	97	86	73
−9	−7	−5	−9	−8	−4
19	38	59	88	78	69

33	51	47	12	72	93
−6	−3	−8	−8	−5	−8
27	48	39	4	67	85

LESSON 86. Regrouping in Subtraction

Purpose: To discover that if there are not sufficient ones when you subtract two 2-place numbers, you must regroup.

Group Activity

Materials: dual board, 10-blocks, cubes, number blocks, two sets of number markers 1 to 9 and 0

- Ask a child to build 52 in the dual board.
- The child puts in 5 tens and 2 ones.
- Write the example on the chalkboard:

    52
    −36

- Elicit that they start with the ones, but cannot subtract because there are only 2 cubes in the ones compartment.
- Say, "You must regroup. Carry back 1 ten to the ones place and exchange it for 10 ones." The child puts 10 single cubes above the 2 cubes to make 12 in all.
- Then say, "12 − 6 = 6" (subtract 6 cubes and leave 6).
- Then the children subtract 3 tens from 4 tens to leave 1 ten.
- The remainder is 16.
- Compute the same example on the chalkboard.

Workbook Page: Go over the illustrations carefully. Have the children work on paper with half-inch squares first. They finish the page independently.

REGROUPING IN SUBTRACTION

A Subtract.

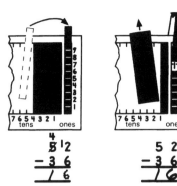

	5 2	4 5̸12	5 2
	−3 6	−3 6	−3 6
		1 6	1 6

Look at the ones. You cannot take 6 ones away from 2 ones. You must regroup.

Carry back 1 ten to the ones column. Exchange 1 ten for 10 ones. Write a small 1 next to the 2. Cross out the 5. Write a 4 above the 5. Subtract.

Do the example.

B
```
 58    67    43    76    21    83
-29   -38   -15   -47   -14   -38
 29    29    28    29     7    45

 95    84    55    97    44    33
-68   -57   -19   -38   -25   -16
 27    27    36    59    19    17
```

LESSON 87. Test

Purpose: To test mastery of regrouping in addition and subtraction.

Group Activity

Note: In this test there are a dozen teen combinations in addition and half a dozen in subtraction which can be reviewed before the test.

Materials: paper, pencils

- Write a different teen number on each child's paper.
- Say, "Make up all the combinations you can think of with this number as the sum."
- Ask the children to subtract from this teen number.
- Ask several children to write their combination in higher decades.
- Give several word problems orally which the children solve by written computation.
  Addition: distance traveled (31 miles + 25 miles + 37 miles)
  total cost of items (15¢ + 25¢ + 57¢)
  number of minutes (30 min. + 15 min. + 25 min.)
  Subtraction: had 90¢ and spent 47¢
  a ribbon was 45 inches long and Ann cut off 17 inches

Workbook Page: Remind the children to observe the plus and minus signs. They finish the page independently.

TEST

A Add or subtract.
```
 29    37    54    38    37    79
+66   +38   -38   +56   -19   +15
 95    75    16    94    18    94

 73    56    67    55    62    85
-47   -48   +26   +27   -17   -67
 26     8    93    82    45    18
```

B Add each example. Check the answers.
```
  6    16    33    18    27     6
  7     8    29    27    20    15
  3    24    10     9    24     7
 +4   +13   +14   +18   +26   +14
 20    61    86    72    97    42
```

C

Jean rode her bike 27 miles to camp. She rode back home the same way.
How many miles did she ride?

    27
  + 27
    54

54 miles

Sue won 80¢ at the fair. She paid 15¢ to take the bus home.
How much money did she have left?

    80
  − 15
    65

Sue had **65**¢ left.

UNIT 15. THE STRUCTURE OF THREE-PLACE NUMBERS

Lessons in this unit:
88. The Structure of Three-Place Numbers
89. Reading and Writing Three-Place Numbers
90. Adding and Subtracting Three-Place Numbers

The Structure of Three-Place Numbers

Grouping ones into tens and tens into hundreds makes computation easier; it keeps the figures we operate with smaller. For example, we do not work with an amount such as 730 days, but call it 2 years. Although *2* stands for a small number, we sense the size, because the word *year* means a long time. It is the same with tens and hundreds. In the number 239, the small numerals stand for big amounts. Children learn to visualize the size of each denomination when they build 3-place numbers with hundred squares, tens, and ones in the dual board.

GAMES AND DEMONSTRATIONS

The First Three-Place Number: 100 (use with Lesson 88)
Materials: dual board, 10-box, ten 10-blocks, ten cubes

- Write two headings on the chalkboard.
      Tens   Ones
- Select a child to record each number on the chalkboard as you build it in the dual board.
- Add (and have the child record) one cube at a time in the ones compartment until there are 10 ones.
- Regroup 10 ones as 1 ten and carry it to the tens compartment. It is recorded as 1 ten, 0 ones.
- Add 1 ten after another until there are 9 tens (recorded as 90). Explain that 9 is the largest number of tens allowed just as 9 ones was the largest number of ones allowed.
- Add ones until there are 9 tens and 9 ones.
- Add 1 cube to 9 tens and 9 ones. Say, "Exchange 10 ones for 1 ten; carry it to the tens place."
- Fill an empty 10-box with the 10 tens and carry it to the hundreds place (to the left of the dual board).
- Show the children that they record this new denomination by placing the number marker for 1 below the hundred square, 0 below the empty tens place, and another 0 below the empty ones place. (The familiar number 100 suddenly has a deeper meaning.) Add a heading for Hundreds on the chalkboard. The child records 1 hundred, 0 tens, 0 ones, and reads the number 100 as "one hundred."
- Children may want to count the units to verify that the total is really 100 ones.
- Explain that we must remove the 10-blocks so we can use them to build other numbers. We will call the 10-box a "hundred square."*

*Set B has five 10-boxes to use as hundreds in building 3-place numbers.

LESSON 88. The Structure of Three-Place Numbers

Purpose: To learn about the structure of 3-place numbers.
Group Activity
Materials: dual board, one 100-square (an empty 10-box), ten 10-blocks, ten cubes, a die with dots 1 to 6
My First Three-Place Number: 100 (see p. 84)
Score One If You Carry
- On the chalkboard write headings for three columns.
    Hundreds   Tens   Ones
- Divide the class into teams A and B; on the chalkboard draw a box in which to write each team's score.
- Team A drops the die and gets 6. A player writes 6 under Ones.
- Team B drops the die and gets 4, adds 4 to 6, announces the sum, and a player writes 1 under Tens and 0 under Ones.
- Since player B has to regroup, or carry over, to the tens column, he scores 1. Write 1 in the score box for team B.
- The winning team is the one with the highest score.

Workbook Page: Go over the pictures carefully. Check the children's ability to read number names. The children finish the page independently.

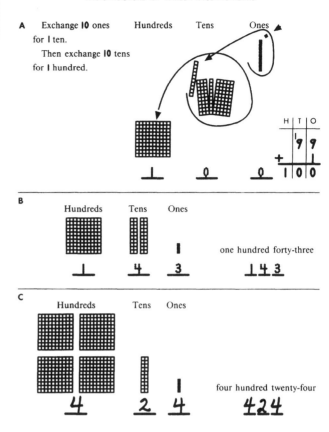

LESSON 89. Reading and Writing Three-Place Numbers

Purpose: To build 3-place numbers and learn to name them, read the names, and record them with numbers.
Group Activity
Materials: dual board, one 100-square (an empty 10-box), ten 10-blocks, ten cubes, paper divided into three columns labeled *hundreds, tens, ones* for each child
- Write a 3-place number in words; ask a child to read it aloud, "One hundred eleven," and record it.
- Have another child build 111 with the materials.
- Give each child a paper.
- Write these numbers on the chalkboard for them to record on their papers:
    three hundred seventeen   one hundred ninety-nine
    one hundred twelve   four hundred eleven
    two hundred eight   nine hundred nine
    five hundred   eight hundred eighteen
    one hundred one   six hundred sixty-six
- Have the children check their numbers by looking at the dual board where a child will build one number after another with the materials.

Workbook Page: A, B, and C. Call on children to read the number names orally. The children finish the page independently.

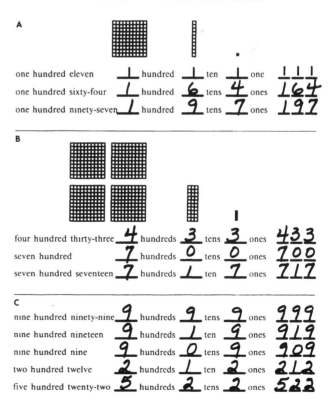

LESSON 90. Adding and Subtracting Three-Place Numbers

Purpose: To teach that in addition or subtraction of 3-place numbers, ones are computed first, then tens, and then hundreds. This lesson does not involve regrouping.

Group Activity

Materials: dual board, five 100-squares, ten 10-blocks, ten cubes

- Write an example on the chalkboard:

    263
    +325

- Child A builds 263 with the materials.
- Child B adds 5 ones to 3 ones, 2 tens to 6 tens, and 3 hundreds to 2 hundreds.
- A child records the total with numbers (588).
- Write a subtraction example on the chalkboard:

    588
    −134

- A child takes 4 cubes from 8, 3 tens from the 8 tens, and 1 hundred from the 5 hundreds; remainder, 454.

Workbook Page: Go over the page carefully. The children finish the page independently.

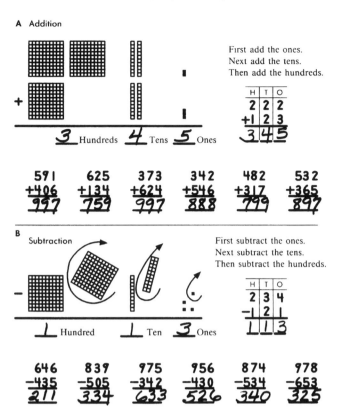

MASTERY TESTS

LESSON 91. Mastery Test

Purpose: To test addition of 2-place numbers that call for regrouping; to solve word problems involving 2-place numbers.

Group Activity
- For children still unsure of the teen facts in addition, review the difficult facts with games. (See Summary of Teen Facts, page 89, for lesson numbers.)

Word Problems in Addition and Subtraction
- On page 28 problems are given for each different type of word problem. To review problem solving for Lessons 91 and 92 make up similar problems using 2-place numbers.
- Present problems in written form or give them orally; let children solve them at the chalkboard.
- Encourage children to make up their own problems (see Lesson 18).

Workbook Page: Caution children to work slowly and think through each example or problem carefully. The children finish the page independently.

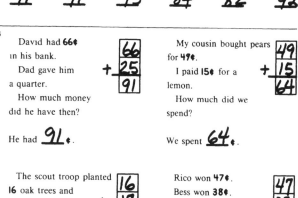

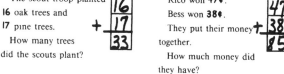

LESSON 92. Mastery Test

Purpose: To test subtraction of 2-place numbers with regrouping; to solve word problems with regrouping.

Group Activity
- For children still unsure of teen facts in subtraction, review difficult facts with games. (See Summary of Teen Facts, page 90, for lesson numbers.)

Subtraction Problems—Which Number Do You Subtract From?

Materials: ten 10-blocks, number blocks 1 to 9

- In the chalk tray display four different 2-place numbers built with 10-blocks and number blocks: 42, 38, 25, 19.
- Say, "I will tell you a subtraction story. I want you to decide which set of blocks you can use to solve it, and then solve it." (Return blocks to the chalk tray after each turn.)
- There were 25 cows in the pen; a hole allowed 19 cows to escape. Which blocks can you use to explain that story?
- There were 42 sheep on the farm; 38 sheep ran away. Which blocks can you use to explain that story?
- Shawn had $19 and spent $15. Which blocks?
- A farmer planted 38 carrots; a rabbit ate 25 of them. Which blocks can you use to explain the story?

Workbook Page: Go over problems of how many more are needed. The children finish the page independently.

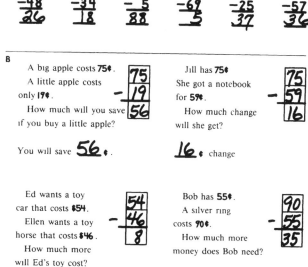

LESSON 93. Mastery Test

Purpose: To test the ability to translate telling time in words to setting hands on a clock face and to the written form; to solve problems involving time.

Group Activity

- For children unsure of telling time on a clock face, review the work by having them set up the materials and play the games described on page 60.

Solving Problems Involving Time

Materials: model clock with gears

- Give a problem in which something begins at a certain time (perhaps 2 o'clock).
- Continue the story: Something goes on for several hours (perhaps 3 hours). At what time does it stop?
- The child takes the minute hand through 3 complete circles (hours) and states the equation, 2 + 3 = 5. It is 5 o'clock when it stops.

Workbook Page: Caution children to work carefully. Go over difficult words ahead of time such as *minute* and *quarter*. The children finish the page independently.

MASTERY TEST

A Mike gets home at 4 o'clock.
He babysits for 2 hours.
What time will he finish?

$$\begin{array}{r}4\\+2\\\hline 6\end{array}$$

He will finish at **6** o'clock.

It takes Mr. Bent 4 hours to mow the lawn.
If he starts at 7 o'clock, when will he finish?

$$\begin{array}{r}7\\+4\\\hline 11\end{array}$$

He will finish at **11** o'clock.

School starts at 9 o'clock.
If the children work 3 hours before lunch, what time do they stop for lunch?

$$\begin{array}{r}9\\+3\\\hline 12\end{array}$$

They stop at **12** o'clock.

Mariko started walking to the lake at 8 o'clock.
She got to the lake after walking 3 hours.
What time did she get there?

$$\begin{array}{r}8\\+3\\\hline 11\end{array}$$

She got there at **11** o'clock.

B Draw the minute hand and write the time.

20 minutes of 4
3:40

a quarter past 7
7:15

a quarter of 3
2:45

9:25

7:30

2:55

LESSON 94. Mastery Test

Purpose: To test addition of 3-place numbers without regrouping; to solve problems involving subtraction or addition for their solution.

Group Activity

Solving Type 3 Problems by Subtraction

- Finding the Rest. Give problems in which there is a total (546 students) and one part is known (223 are boys). The children are asked to find the rest: How many are girls? (546 − 223 = 323) 323 are girls.
- Finding How Many More. Give problems in which a total is stated (150 books) and a certain part of the job is finished (50 books have been packed). The children are asked to find how many more still need to be packed. (150 − 50 = 100) 100 more books.
- Finding the Difference. Give problems in which two amounts are stated (206 pandas, 213 elephants). The children are asked to find the difference, either how many more elephants or how many fewer pandas. (213 − 206 = 7) 7 more elephants.

Workbook Page: The children finish the test independently.

MASTERY TEST

A There are 546 children in the Field School.
In June, 105 children went on a trip to the zoo.
How many children were left in school?

$$\begin{array}{r}546\\-105\\\hline 441\end{array}$$

441 children

The bus driver went 264 miles before lunch.
After lunch she went 104 miles.
How many miles did she go that day?

$$\begin{array}{r}264\\+104\\\hline 368\end{array}$$

She went **368** miles.

If you drive on Route 7, it is 339 miles to Rochester.
If you take a short cut, it is 307 miles.
How much shorter is the short cut?

$$\begin{array}{r}339\\-307\\\hline 32\end{array}$$

32 miles

Abe's book is 358 pages long.
He is on page 127.
How many more pages does Abe have left to read?

$$\begin{array}{r}358\\-127\\\hline 231\end{array}$$

231 more pages

B

564	274	402	335	487
+304	+605	+597	+622	+312
868	879	999	957	799

542	363	125	603	427
+325	+325	+634	+384	+340
867	688	759	987	767

SUMMARY OF TEEN FACTS IN ADDITION

The following brief summaries outline how the teen facts in addition are taught in *Structural Arithmetic II*. Because the facts described in each group are structurally related, children can master them by understanding one generalization. For students who have not yet mastered these facts, review by playing the games in the appropriate lesson(s).

Structurally Related Groups of Facts

Adding to 9 (Lesson 55). In the 20-tray build the stair from 1 to 20. First add a block to 10 (10 + 7 = 17); then add the same block to 9 (9 + 7 is only 16). Adding a number to 9 gives an answer 1 less than if the same number had been added to 10.

Adding 9 (Lesson 63). In the number track add 10 to a number; the sum has the same ones digit in the next decade (7 + 10 = 17). Adding 9 to a number yields a sum that is 1 less than if 10 had been added to that number (7 + 9 = 16).

Adding to 8 (Lesson 56). In the number track add a number block to 10 (10 + 7 = 17); then add the same block to 8 (8 + 7 = 15). Adding a number to 8 gives an answer 2 less than if the same number had been added to 10.

Adding 8 (Lesson 64). In the number track add 10 to a number; the sum has the same ones digit in the next higher decade (7 + 10 = 17). Adding 8 to a number is 2 less than if 10 had been added to that number (7 + 8 = 15).

Combinations That Make 11 (Lesson 68). Build the stair from 1 to 10 in the 20-tray. Add blocks to make the combinations with a sum of 10. Move the top stair of blocks up 1 step. This yields the combinations with a sum of 11.

Combinations That Make 12 (Lesson 70). The numbers that are opposite each other on the face of the clock make 12 when added together. Build the stair from 1 to 10 in the 20-tray. Add the blocks to make the combinations with a sum of 10. Move the top stair of blocks up 2 steps. This yields the combinations with a sum of 12.

Doubles (Lesson 72). In the doubles and neighbors board put in the even number markers 12, 14, 16, 18, and 20. Above each sum put the blocks for the doubles 6 + 6, 7 + 7, 8 + 8, 9 + 9, and 10 + 10.

Neighbors (Lesson 73). In the doubles and neighbors board put in place the odd number markers 11, 13, 15, 17, and 19. Above each sum put in two blocks that are neighbors (consecutive numbers): 5 + 6, 6 + 7, 7 + 8, 8 + 9, and 9 + 10.

TEEN FACTS IN ADDITION

Structurally Related Facts
- Adding 9 / Adding to 9
- Adding 8 / Adding to 8
- Diagonal: Combinations that make 11
- Diagonal: Combinations that make 12
- ■ Doubles
- ☐ Neighbors (consecutive numbers)

SUMMARY OF TEEN FACTS IN SUBTRACTION

The following brief summaries outline how the teen facts in subtraction are taught in *Structural Arithmetic II*. Because the facts described in each group are structurally related, children can master them by understanding one generalization. For students who have not yet mastered these facts, review by playing the games in the appropriate lesson(s).

Structurally Related Groups of Facts

Subtracting 9 (Lesson 65). In the number track build a teen number such as 3 + 10; from 13 take 10; this leaves 3. Now add blocks 1 + 9 to the 3-block. This time subtract 9; the remainder is 3 + 1, or 4. When 9 is subtracted from a number, the answer is 1 more than if 10 had been subtracted from that number.

Remainder of 9 (Lesson 75). In the number track build 13 using blocks 9 + 1 and 3. Now subtract blocks 3 + 1; the remainder is 9. To get a remainder of 9 you must subtract a number 1 more than the ones digit.

Remainder of 8 (Lesson 75). In the number track build 13 using blocks 8 + 2 and 3. Think, 13 − 3 = 10. Now subtract blocks 3 + 2; the remainder is 8. To get a remainder of 8, you subtract a number 2 more than the ones digit.

Subtracting from 11 (Lesson 69). In the number track place two blocks that have a sum of 11, such as 7 and 4. First demonstrate that 11 − 4 = 7 and then that 11 − 7 = 4.

Subtracting from 12 (Lesson 71). In the number track place two blocks that have the sum of 12, such as 7 + 5. First demonstrate that 12 − 5 = 7, and then that 12 − 7 = 5.

Subtracting from Doubles (Lesson 74). In the doubles and neighbors board put the number markers 12, 14, 16, 18, and 20 and the blocks for the doubles 6 + 6, 7 + 7, 8 + 8, 9 + 9, and 10 + 10. Subtracting one part of a double leaves the other (14 − 7 = 7).

Subtracting from Sums of Neighbors (Consecutive Numbers) (Lesson 74). In the doubles and neighbors board put the number markers for the odd numbers 11, 13, 15, 17, and 19. Fill the board with pairs of consecutive number blocks: 5 + 6, 6 + 7, 7 + 8, 8 + 9, 9 + 10. Cover a pair of blocks; subtracting one part leaves the other (15 − 7 = 8 or 15 − 8 = 7).

100-Square

Cut out this square and glue it to the inside of an extra 10-box.

Made in the USA
San Bernardino, CA
07 May 2014